Unlocking the Rhythms of Grace

DISCOVER HOW TO PARTNER WITH GOD
IN A NEW WAY FOR YOUR NEXT SEASON.

Patrick A. Hegarty

HEGARTY.COM.AU

AUSTRALIA

Unlocking the Rhythms of Grace

Copyright © 2016 Patrick Hegarty.

All rights reserved. No part of this publication may be reproduced, distributed or transmitted in any form or by any means, including photocopying, recording, or other electronic or mechanical methods, without the prior written permission of Patrick Hegarty, except in the case of brief quotations embodied in critical reviews and certain other noncommercial uses permitted by copyright law. For permission requests, email the author, with subject line "Attention: Permissions Enquiry" at the email address below.

info@hegarty.com.au

www.hegarty.com.au

Scriptures quoted from:
New International Version of the Bible. Scripture taken from the Holy Bible, NEW INTERNATIONAL VERSION®. Copyright ©1973, 1978, 1984 International Bible Society. All rights reserved throughout the world. Used by permission of International Bible Society.

Scripture quotations identified MSG are from The Message. Copyright © 1993, 1994, 1995 by Eugene Peterson. Used by permission of NavPress Publishing Group.

Any internet addresses (websites, blogs, etc.) in this book are offered as a resources. They are not intended in any way to be or imply an endorsement by Patrick Hegarty, nor does Patrick Hegarty vouch for the content of these sites for the life of this book.

Unlocking the Rhythms of Grace/ Patrick A. Hegarty. —1st ed.
ISBN 978-1-888810-75-2

Praise for this book

I didn't know people still wrote books like this anymore!

In "Unlocking the Rhythms of Grace," Pat has written a deep but highly accessible exploration of what it means to know God and to serve Him truly.

This is not a book to read in a hurry; it's a book to slowly and thoughtfully ponder, praying continuously through it page by page. If you do that – over the four-week period for which it is written – your life will be transformed!

On one hand, Pat does not give you a quick-fix formula for spiritual growth. On the other hand, if you will give yourself to the simple biblical principles Pat so beautifully outlines here, it will work! You will be changed, day by day, more and more into Jesus' image.

Pat's great work, "Unlocking the Rhythms of Grace" will give you tremendous help as you grow in the Spirit and Word of the Living God.

Malcolm Webber, Ph.D.
Founder and Executive Director
LeaderSource SGA

Contents

Get the most out of this book xi
Introduction xiii

Breathing on Dust 1
Room to Breathe 11
Moments of Transition 21
Walking with God 33
Working with God 43
Faith Foundations 53
Spirit and Truth 63
Faith to Walk 73
Faith to Work 84
Igniting the Engine of Faith 94
A Hopeful Mind 103
An Engine of Change 114
Repenting of Religion 124
Believing for Today 133
Believing for Tomorrow 143
Primary Love 153
Faith and Deeds 163
Seasonal Assignments 172
Rest for the Weary 181
Crossing Jordan 191

To my wife Trish

You are noble beyond all others (Proverbs 31:10).

We are becoming who we will be — forever.

—Dallas Willard, The Divine Conspiracy

Get the most out of this book

DIG DEEPER INTO INDIVIDUAL RHYTHMS OF GRACE

THIS BOOK IS DESIGNED as an overview, introducing some of the core principles for each Rhythm of Grace. To apply the concepts more fully, there is a growing library of resources available for individuals, groups, and churches. Visit the website at: www.HEGARTY.com.au.

DOWNLOAD THE FREE JOURNAL AND GROUP NOTES

PRINT OUT THE COMPANION Journal and Group Notes for this book at www.hegarty.com.au. Write down your thoughts as you process the principles and questions daily.

Use a Format that Fits in with Your Life

PRINCIPLES ARE BEST DIGESTED when you are free to think independently. The daily content is available in multiple formats including print, digital, and even audio.

Digest the Ideas Daily

AVOID READING MORE THAN one chapter per day. The principles within each chapter are best applied if you give yourself time to think them through fully.

Work it Through with Some Friends

MAXIMIZE THE BENEFITS OF this book by working it through with friends or as a whole church. The group notes will refer to your daily journal responses as part of the group meeting.

Introduction

BEFORE I WAS A senior pastor, I invested over a decade in a very specific pastoral role called Spiritual Development. Having come out of a career in engineering and business, I was drawn to investigate and cooperate with how God moulded people into their best version of themselves.

The church of around three thousand regular attendees was large enough to allow me time to experiment and learn from God's "creative sandbox." I wanted to find out how people really grew in their faith, and how it was that many did not. Just as importantly ... why they did not.

Over the years, thousands of Christians attended our retreats and courses. I wrote over a million words of content and led scores of groups. Along the way, my team and I made a few mistakes. But we also discovered some new ideas that completely changed the way we looked at discipleship.

We saw many hundreds of jaw-dropping examples of lives revolutionised by Jesus. Ordinary disciples were set on fire for God, spiritual gifts were released, bodies and hearts were healed, missionaries were sent, and all sorts of ministries were initiated – all the things a pastor longs to see.

> **We saw many hundreds of jaw-dropping examples of lives revolutionised by Jesus**

I will never forget the names of these renewed lives ... or their stories. Like the wealthy but spiritually jaded businessman, confronted like the Apostle Paul with the power and presence of Jesus, so convicted that he purchased a minivan so he could personally visit and feed those living on the streets. Or the stoic mathematics genius who became so enamoured with grace that he would travel for hours on the city rail network looking for people he could pray for. And the broken-hearted young woman who had left God and country to indulge in the worst of lives, who became so transformed by an experience of God's love that she gave her whole life to releasing that awesome love to others.

I also saw some confounding examples of people who remained stagnated in their faith. Fear, bitterness, cynicism and a myriad of other negative symptoms strangled their logic and hope. There were two main categories within this group: those who were stuck, and those who went stale.[1]

---

[1] This finding correlated to the comprehensive research of Willow Creek Community Church in Chicago in their world-wide spiritual health surveys, as summarised in the "Reveal" series. In particular: Hawkins Greg L. & Parkinson Cally (2007), *Reveal Where Are You?*, Willow Creek Association.

Those who were stuck seemed to have their spiritual feet shackled to their past. For whatever reason, they could not or would not take the step of maturity to become the *pnuematikos*, the spirit-empowered person.[2] They remained largely defeated and unable to move forward.

The stale group was comprised predominantly of mature Christians who had either become disillusioned with church life, or simply bored through being under-challenged in their spirituality. Their passion had waned, and they were investing the best of their creative energies in career or hobbies rather than pursuing new possibilities for God's glory.

The Simple Key to Breakthrough

By God's grace over the years, I discovered that if anyone was open to being "unstuck," there was a simple and powerful solution available. Don't get me wrong; there is not a "one size fits all" solution. The solution was definitely not the same for everyone, but each solution was nonetheless simple!

It wasn't just a change of habit or a new book that these people needed. Nor did they require a high-voltage, heart-starting jolt from the Spirit of God. They needed a simple dynamic that incorporated all of those components. They needed a new way to partner with God in a transformational season.

---

[2] *Pnuematikos*, translated in First Corinthians 3:1, refers to the spiritual person, or one who lives by the Spirit.

> **They needed a new way to partner with God in a transformational season**

Time and again, I saw that God wanted to change the way the relationship was working in these folks' lives. He was longing to add new layers of interaction and empowerment. God was offering an upgrade to the partnership, but to embrace it they would need to hang on to Him a little tighter!

Once I caught on to this biblical idea of partnership with God, it released an avalanche of ideas and environments. The sheer amount of material I had produced took me some time to work through, but I eventually gathered together the principles that had worked. I then deconstructed them to discover why they worked.

The one irrefutable conclusion that kept coming up was that God could revive absolutely anyone! We had burned-out pastors, crusty Bible college lecturers, stoic surgeons, pharisaic prosecutors, tired mothers, cynical graduates, and hardened executives ... and they all experienced significant transformation. It seems that no one was "safe" from the transforming power of God!

God wants to get hold of you, too, and bring you into a more abundant life. If you are willing to put each element of your life on the table for God to arrange as He wills, and to bow your heart to His, then you are positioned for an upgrade. By making all of our life accessible to His hands, we make room for God to do what only He can do – renovate the human soul.

False Binaries Exposed

I came to realize that man had separated what God had put together. All we had to do – all we have to do – is re-join them! I am referring to the false divide that denominationalism inadvertently fosters. By attracting groups of people with similar beliefs and preferences of worship, the typical local church inadvertently portrays a quite one-sided expression.

> *I came to realize that man had separated what God had put together*

Being correct and strong in one area often conspires to prevent the possibility of embracing the complementary strength. For example, the conservatives gather to the left, and the charismatics to the right. Both have strong elements of truth, and yet both lack the strength that the other could add.

Again, you might find contemplatives on the left, and the social justice advocates on the right. Neither quite "gets" the other, and sadly there remains a tension where there could be a fusion.

But what if you could go further than merely finding an awkward middle position between two ends of a supposed spectrum? What if you could actually embrace both fully?

What if Spirit and Truth could be held in the same high value? What if we could be just as strong in walking with God as we are in working with God?

As I began to crystalize these ideas, I realized that to better embrace these various elements, I needed to change the way I viewed the differences. Previously, I thought in binary or polarised terms. I would put two seemingly opposing views at each end of a line and determine what the best position was between them.

For example, I had been taught that there were word-centred people and spirit-centred people. We each had to decide where we sat on that spectrum. However, this is a false binary! We need to fully embrace truth, and fully embrace the Spirit. To do any less would require us to completely re-write the New Testament.

I found a number of these false binaries as I looked deeper into what God was doing in our midst. And I learned that God had not just re-joined the things that we separate, He actually used them to feed into each other!

Dwelling with God's Spirit was actually leading people to hunger for God's Word! Discovering more truth was in turn fuelling hunger for more of God's empowering presence. Spiritual engines were being ignited – releasing those who were stuck, and envisioning those who were stale.

I began to think in terms of cycles instead of spectrums. And it soon became apparent that I was on to something!

The Rhythms of Grace

The Message version of the Bible has a wonderful way of translating Matthew 11:28-30:

> Are you tired? Worn out? Burned out on religion? Come to me. Get away with me and you'll recover your life. I'll show you how to take a real rest. Walk with me and work with me—watch how I do it. Learn the unforced rhythms of grace.

Most of the "stuck" people I was confronting in my ministry had simply become worn out. They were either defeated or disillusioned by what they had experienced in life and church. The solution Jesus' offers is to draw near to Him, and to watch what He does as we walk and work with Him.

He doesn't expect us to either walk or work. We need to do both because both are true and necessary. We can't simply retreat to the mountains indefinitely and pray. Nor can we exhaust ourselves in un-empowered labour. Each must have its moment and be allowed to give fuel to the other in turn.

> ***His tangible presence alone gives us what we cannot give ourselves***

There is a rhythm to follow, the cadence of which is unique to each of us. What is common to both, however, is the need for God's grace. His tangible presence alone gives us what we cannot give ourselves.

In this book, I have highlighted four unique "rhythms" of grace. The overarching rhythm is that of Walking and Working. All the others run in synchronicity with this. We are to extend and retreat – push forward and pull back.

The other three rhythms are like spiritual engines. They run on the fuel of a surrendered heart, and output unique fruit such as faith, hope, and love.

All the engines can easily run all of the time; their pace is unforced once you get to know them. But there are specific moments throughout our spiritual journey where emphasis on one of the rhythms can catalyse a significant shift in our fruitfulness and vision.

This book serves as an introduction. Each five-day week is dedicated to one rhythm of grace. From there you can decide if any particular spiritual engine needs to be reignited.

Enjoy walking and working with God!

[1.1]

Breathing on Dust

HOW DO YOU RESPOND when you read the New Testament description of life with God? Can you imagine actually seeing seas calmed, bodies healed, thousands saved, prisoners released, and the proud knocked off their high-horse? Can you imagine Christ reaching out to you, with hands of healing and words of grace? No doubt the biblical narrative represents a highlight reel of sorts, but the reality is that throughout history God makes a point of invading our lives in big and small ways.

Would you not love to see a little more of that for yourself? Or maybe the big stuff is beyond your hopes, and you would be happy with nothing more than a tangible sense of God's presence and peace.

Some days you probably look up from your Bible and consider the gap between the disciples' stories and yours. Right now you are possibly looking down the barrel of a daily grind with endless demands on time, a need to constantly produce income, a lack of rest, career challenges, a body that won't cooperate, the need to be a "perfect parent," and on it goes.

Will you have to wait for heaven to witness some real power, meaning, or even time with God?

Thousands of times I have had this same conversation with individuals and groups. After asking about their own experience of engagement with Jesus, the themes that leak out are usually much the same. They go something like this:

> "I just don't have time to press in to God. There are too many demands on my time."

> "It was easier back in Jesus' day; they didn't have the schedule we do."

> "You can't be a spiritual mystic and also engage in the real world ... we need to get things done."

> "I am just not like that; only the truly exceptional get to see God do those things like He did in the Bible."

> "I used to be engaged in church and ministry, but it left me dry. I 'died to self' so much it almost killed me."

This is the talk of good-hearted but struggling Christians who have endured spiritual dehydration for so long they can't even recognise their barrenness. They have settled for a life so far from what God genuinely offers that they believe it can't exist for them.

Dust + Breath

Spiritual powerlessness and emotional dryness. They are so pervasive that now we have largely accepted them as normal. But if we are to accept them, we are also obliged to rewrite our theology, philosophy of life, and spiritual expectations. We must also mould our lives around sustaining that debilitating reality, ensuring such a life and belief system makes sense, lest we feel guilty as well as dry.

In that arid version of reality, only half of the creation narrative in Genesis 2:7 makes sense – the part where God formed us from the dust of the earth. That half-verse confirms largely how we feel ... dusty and devoid of spiritual life.

And yet there is a second half to that verse ... God Himself breathed life into us, and only at that point did we became alive. If we are not experiencing His Spirit daily, we are living at best a half-life.

> **Life without an experience of the Spirit is a half-life**

Profoundly, Jesus breathed on the disciples after His resurrection, saying, "Receive the Spirit."[1] Through our newly restored relationship with God that Jesus' sacrifice enabled,

---

[1] John 20:22

access to spiritual life was again made available. Now we are new creations, the original order of dust + breath restored.

Jesus had earlier promised that rivers of living water would flow from within us, and also declared that God gives the Spirit without limit.[2] The overarching theme we see here is that where God's breath is, there is also tangible life. Without it, there is not.

But since so few actually seem to experience that life, we might feel obliged to re-scope the definition of what Jesus actually meant. We figure He must have meant that this experience is for later, in heaven.

Not so.

Take a closer look at the creation narrative. The source of our being is also that which sustains us on earth.

The water brought forth creatures, and they continued to draw life from that same sea.[3] The earth brought forth land creatures who were designed to live from those same sustaining elements.[4]

Humanity was born of both dust of the earth and the breath of God. The reality is that we are meant to draw from the nutrients of this earth, and from the Spirit of God who

---

[2] John 7:38; John 3:34
[3] Genesis 1:20 (KJV)
[4] Genesis 1:24 (KJV)

breathes life into our being.[5] We are people of both earth and heaven. According to our design, we can only experience true life when we draw from both realities.

When we work, we should be aware of – and draw from – God's grace and power. Likewise when we rest, we should not assume that we need to disengage or merely escape life. Rest is about engaging with God to feed our soul, rather than merely escaping reality.

God's presence is always available, but the real issue is that most of us aren't sure how to draw on that life in the midst our current circumstance.

> **God's presence is available ... but we aren't sure how to draw on that life**

Doing and Being

Western Christian culture has created a binary view on existing with God that on the surface seems to fit with the idea of dust and breath. We talk in terms of doing and being, separating into boxes these two elements of life.

We see doing as our actual activity – getting things done, thinking up answers, doing the work of life and advancing the kingdom. Some people would go so far as to even call themselves "doers."

---

[5] Romans 8:11

Being, on the other hand, is seen as focussing on self-awareness and acceptance. It is viewed as inner-world activity where there is reflection and relationship with God.

The two seem to be mutually exclusive. Depending on our profile and history, we might gravitate to one preference more than the other. We may even argue that those in the "other camp" are actually missing the point, even providing scriptural back-up for our view.

The challenge with this worldview is that God largely seems to dwell in only in the "being" box. We engage with Him in the hope that that He tops us up enough to get through our day of "doing." We form an unconscious divide in our life between our secular and sacred spaces. Our vocation and activity are secular, and our devotional life is defined as sacred, and the two struggle to have a realistic impact on each other.

And yet we are designed of both dust and breath. The two are so intrinsically mixed together that they cannot be separated into sacred and secular. All of our life is meant to be a partnership between us and God. We shouldn't attempt to separate our inner and outer worlds from fellowship with God. He is all and is in all.[6]

Something within us knows that there is a time to rest and a time to get up and do something. There is a rhythm to life we are created to enjoy. What we don't realise is that

---

[6] Colossians 3:11

every part of that rhythm can be enjoyed in partnership with God.

We don't need to separate that which God has put together. What we need is a way to grow in our capacity to live out the promised joy, peace, power, and rest of New Testament life. And since God gives the Spirit without limit, we know the problem of supply is not at His end.

A way to explain this is more easily seen when we replace the words doing and being with walking and working. And rather than have them at opposite ends of a spectrum, we need to join them in a cycle. In this way each of the elements leads into and enhances the other, rather than trying to oppose or at best balance each other out.

God partners with us in both elements. He walks with us and He works with us. And it is all done through a rhythm that brings abundant life.

Extend and Release

The worldview that divides doing and being wears us down, but this idea of walking and working does the opposite. It grows our capacity to engage with and draw from God.

You can see this dynamic at work in many other areas of life, the most obvious being with physical exercise. Elite athletes do not exercise constantly without a break. They extend and release. They push hard, but then they rest well.

They understand the dynamic of recreation in the process of capacity growth. To grow in muscle capacity, they design a workout that forces the muscle to perform for short periods at a level way beyond its normal sustainable output. This interval of extension actually tears down the muscle fibres as it exerts unsustainable output.

> **Both extend and release phases are vital for growth**

Because of this, the athlete must rest that muscle for one or two days. This is the rest phase where the muscle literally re-creates itself – which is where the word recreation comes from. By repeating this cycle for a period of six to eight weeks, the body begins to command the muscle to adapt to this extra load by building more tissue. The result is that the new "normal" for the muscle is higher than before.

Both extend and release phases are vital for growth.

In regard to growing our capacity to engage with the unlimited grace of God, we can use the same principle. God designed us to apply spiritually the same principle we apply physically. We grow through adopting the rhythm of walking and working.

Look again at Jesus' offer to those dry and dusty souls that walked past Him daily:

"Are you tired? Worn out? Burned out on religion? Come to me. Get away with me and you'll recover your life. I'll show you how to take a real rest. Walk with me and work with me—watch how I do it. Learn the unforced rhythms of grace" (Matthew 11:28-30 – MSG).

Grace, which has been defined by theologian Gordon Fee as "God's empowering presence,"[7] is with us as we walk and work with Him in this rhythm of grace. It is unforced and natural.

There is a specific cadence to this rhythm that will work for you. We are all different, and yet we all need to practice some degree of rest as well as extension. If we focus on just one of these, ultimately we will revert to our own strength in that area. A constant flat-line of activity that does not experience rest will eventually result in a flat-line in our heart.

> *There is a specific cadence to this rhythm that will work for you*

Is that you?

Have you flat-lined? Have you simply been working for God without knowing how to work with God?

Have you felt permission to be one who can both be and do?

---

[7] Fee, Gordon D. (2009) *God's Empowering Presence*. Baker Publishing Group.

How long has it been since you experienced God's grace tangibly effecting your levels of strength, enthusiasm, impact, creativity, and mercy?

Too long, I suspect. You deserve better. You were designed for better.

This material will help you break out of the stagnating equilibrium of life so you can experience the thrilling rate-of-change that comes from experiencing new things with God. It will challenge the way you think, but once you grasp hold of God's rhythms of grace, your current idea of normal may begin to appear a little underwhelming. Your efforts will bear more fruit, and your rest will become re-creation.

Your Response:

How have you managed to find balance between the demands of your life, and your ability to rest in God? Do your days and weeks have a rhythm where you oscillate from output to input? Or do you perhaps feel like you have flat-lined in to a life of constant output? How would you describe your levels of rest?

[1.2]

Room to Breathe

THERE IS AN ELEMENT of genius in God's design that ensures living beings must breathe. The brilliant idea is that we don't just breathe once; we must do it continually.

Have you ever tried to exhale and then tried to go about your duties without inhaling again? Obviously, this practice would have a limited shelf-life.

The spiritual parallel is no less vital than the physical one. The original words for "spirit" in both the Old and New Testaments are the same as "breath." We are made to literally breathe God in, receiving grace for life. And we are also to breathe out, releasing His grace to a dusty world.

There should be a natural rhythm to this, since both phases of the cycle are incomplete until they activate the next.

Take a quick spiritual health check on this now – how is the rhythm of your spiritual breathing? Do you spend a lot more than you receive? Most people would say yes. They are far more aware of the spiritual and emotional withdrawals in their life than they are of God's deposits. This can be quite frustrating, especially for those dutiful ones who withdraw regularly for a time of quiet devotion. It is almost like they are turning up at the fuel station but never quite getting gas in the tank.

> **We are far more aware of life's withdrawals than we are of God's deposits**

This sense of lack is most frequently caused by us seeking something from God that He is not necessarily releasing. When Jesus offered rest to the weary in Matthew 11:28, the rest was in the form of Himself. He invited us to come directly to Him – to engage with Him. Normally when we enter a time of prayer and devotion, it takes the form of a list that we hope God will answer – our rest being somewhat reliant on those answers coming forth.

Having led spiritual retreats for many years, I find the most common blockage to people actually engaging powerfully with God is their own agenda. They come looking for God to either fix something, or to give them some form of experience. Often the answer they seek is frustratingly within reach, as they endure watching the person right next to them experience God in the way they were hoping to.

Yet the person who experienced God so manifestly is often the person who hadn't sought an experience at all. They were simply hungering for Jesus. They were content in their walk, yet came with expectancy that anything was possible. The frustrated ones were more often those who came not with expectancy, but with expectation – they had a defined outcome in mind.

Too often our priority is to have our needs to be met by Jesus, yet we are first called to have them met in Jesus.

Our ability to engage with God at this level, literally breathing in His grace constantly – walking with Him and working with Him – is the single greatest principle to living a life of peace, grace, and impact.

> *We are first called to have our needs met in Jesus, rather than by Jesus*

The myth that lies so close to this truth, however, is that in order to foster a level of intimacy, you must hunker down to a life of monastic prayer – becoming separate from the world. The practice of separation may protect the relationship you have with Jesus now, but it won't allow you to grow. And God is determined that you grow!

A Developmental Need

If you enjoy a routine of physical exercise such as running, you will understand that there are multiple elements to our physical capacity. To go faster, we need muscles to be developed further. If those muscles can't be supplied with oxygen at the rate congruent with their capacity, the heart and lungs become the cap of performance.

Again, the physical dynamic here also reflects the spiritual one. Rather than give you rest, you may find that your life in Christ actually increase the demands on your life. The momentum of activity, fellowship, ministry, and worship normally continues to increase as you stay engaged in local church life. This is on top of all the other components of life that we share with our un-churched neighbours. We still have our careers, homes, families, and friends to engage with.

> **Spiritual maturity is determined by your capacity to walk and work with God**

With this stifling combination, you may soon find it hard to breathe! Be clear on one thing, however – this is a life that is growing in busyness, not necessarily in spiritual health. Unless you have let go deliberately, all the luggage from your past is still on a trolley being pulled along behind you. The fact that you are a new creation in Christ does not imply that your memory banks are clear and your mind is thinking clearly.

There are significant stages of spiritual growth to get through on your journey to becoming all that you are created to be. These stages are not defined by your Christian activity;

they are defined by the state of your inner world, and your capacity to walk and work with God.

Most of us are not taught this in our discipleship classes. We are encouraged to get connected and get involved – to play our part sacrificially and love each other sincerely. Meanwhile, if we aren't aware, our inner world begins to suffocate. We cannot keep up!

Our activity begins to over-reach our capacity. Even the time we set aside for God can feel like another box to tick on that ever-growing list of expectations. Meanwhile, our thought life still harbours the same old judgments, anxiety, and lusts that it always did.

Of course, the list of burdens just keeps growing. We are still trying to bear the pressures of a world where standards of appearance and performance continue to soar beyond realism. Social media throws a constant stream of posed selfies at us – the "perfect-parent" syndrome ensures I can't share my failures. I feel increasingly isolated because my church profile now prohibits me from being honest about my sin. Shame management and fear of failure increase my internal stress levels to the breaking point!

> *Like swans we glide by gracefully while under the surface we are paddling like mad*

All this can be happening while our outer world appears to be going so well. Like a swan on the lake, we glide by gracefully while under the surface we are paddling like mad.

No wonder we are spiritually breathless.

We need to find practical ways to increase our capacity to deal with these issues and to actually breathe spiritually again. If we don't, we either stall in our faith, begin to suffer symptoms of anxiety, or join the increasing majority of people who profess a faith but can longer exist in a church setting.

Two Kings

King Saul started well enough. His story is chronicled in the book of First Samuel. He hadn't wanted to be king but soon embraced it with gusto. But his life's demands began to exceed his spiritual capacity. As we will see, the pressure exerted by our "outer world" circumstances will always result in an implosion back to the capacity of our "inner world."

Saul's enemy had him overwhelmingly outnumbered as he awaited a battle at Gilgal. Men were deserting him and fear gripped his heart. Where was Samuel the prophet? Saul had been told to meet Samuel there and wait so they could sacrifice to God, but time was running out. The pressure was greater than Saul's faith in both God and His prophet, so he decided to take the initiative. Saul was in trouble, but his real failure was that he didn't take a breath.

Saul conducted the sacrificial ceremony that Samuel was supposed to perform, hoping to garner God's favour. Sadly, his action was a significant over-reach of authority, and it effectively disqualified him from fulfilling his calling. His life was never the same. His story became a tale of fear, jealousy, and rage against God's purposes.

When Samuel arrived and saw what Saul had done, he prophesied at that moment that God had someone else in mind. This new king would grow to fulfil all that God had for the nation. His choice was a young man who shared the very heart of God – David.[1]

David was not only a warrior; he was also a worshipper. His work for God was an overflow of his walk with God. For years he had sat with his lyre, singing and enjoying the companionship of God. Safe under the wings of the Faithful One, David could only grow in faith.

> **His work for God was an overflow of his walk with God**

He came to public prominence when his heart came to the surface, not just his skills. As he heard Goliath trash-talk the God he loved, David could not remain passive. His ears could not tolerate the blasphemy because his love for God was so strong in his core. Either Goliath was about to die, or David was, simply because he could not exist in the presence of such slander.[2]

---

[1] 1 Samuel 13:14
[2] 1 Samuel 17

You know how the story ends – the passion of David's heart combined with a single smooth stone ended the day in David's favour. And in God's.

Making Room to Breathe

This was only the start for David, however. He had to grow in the capacity required to avoid the errors of his predecessor, so God called him into a wilderness of experience. There, he would grow his spiritual lungs for fourteen years or so through trials and unreasonable pressure that threatened to snuff him out.

Yet David remained empowered by the heart of God, writing through those years, "The Lord is my shepherd, I lack nothing. He makes me lie down in green pastures, He leads me beside quiet waters, He refreshes my soul."[3]

> **David continued to morph his ability to breathe spiritually**

He was a man of violence, prone to sin, and capable of terrible decisions. Yet David overcame it all to be the greatest king Israel would have. He even grew to become an Old Testament pointer towards Christ Himself.

David had continued to morph his ability to breathe spiritually as each level of maturity progressed. He gave himself permission to rest. He spoke to his own soul, telling

---

[3] Psalm 23:1-3

himself to hope in God alone rather than in the outcome of his challenges. He recognised his tendencies to fail, bringing his shortcomings before God in transparency. David was real before God.

The core difference between the two kings was their ability to rely on and work with God. They both started well ... but only one navigated the pathway of developing his internal world to match his calling.

The rhythms of grace are a way to describe this ability to increasingly inhale and exhale the grace of God. As you continue along your own journey, there are strategic moments where you need to walk to a new rhythm. As you are confronted with each challenge to grow, you will stand at a fork in the road. You can choose to partner with God in a new way, or you can attempt to go it alone as you try to do the new things your life will require in all the strength you can muster.

> *The rhythms of grace are a way to describe this ability to increasingly inhale and exhale the grace of God*

God will not force your hand; the choices remain yours. Yet there is no entry into the promised land of your calling without the sufficient tools of faith.

I know you want to walk and work with God. That is why you are still reading. I am happy to share with you the principles of this journey throughout the rest of this short book. I have had the pleasure of leading thousands of people through this path. I know that you, too, will learn to breathe as you are created to.

You were designed to live, not merely exist. Your spiritual lungs were created for grace – it is time to let them breathe.

Your Response:

Have you had moments along your journey of faith where you became aware that your inner walk with God is not keeping up with the demands of your life? If so, what caused you to over-reach in that way?

[1.3]

Moments of Transition

HOW DO YOU TAKE the joy, peace, power, and boldness from the pages of the Book of Acts and weave it in to your own story?

How do you move on from a life of talking about God, to one where you talk with God?

How do you exchange fear, sadness, and anger – for faith, hope, and love?

These are the questions that all of us should confront. Some, through the pain of their disappointment, believe that they can't breakthrough into these things. And yet some others have walked with God in such a way that faith, hope, and love are indeed their story.

They are the overcomers. The journey of breakthrough continues for them daily, but through the midst of failure and challenge they continue to experience the joy of forgiveness, power, and grace in ever-increasing measure. This is your calling too.

The past need not be the blueprint for your future. If you can understand some of the basic principles of growing in Christ, the road ahead can continue as it should towards your own true north. Failure to do so will send you off track, to circumnavigate the same mountains year after year.

To explain some of the key points of the journey, and how to transition into them, I invite you into some of my own story. The main reason I have seen a degree of success in growing others is because God set me on an intensive journey of radical change for over twenty years. The lessons I learned in that period can serve you well, saving you many years of unnecessary pain and delay.

An Early Breakthrough in Faith

I was raised in an atheistic home in the rougher parts of a big city. My father had died tragically when I was only months old, compelling my grieving mother to work hard at becoming educated and trained as a clinical nurse. That vocation led to a career of irregular shifts and something of a broken rhythm at home.

Most of my childhood was spent in my own company, feeding a growing introversion and starving my spirit of the joy of interacting with many people. Aloneness fostered insecurity. As I grew, I became increasing aware that I had no idea who I really was. What I did know of myself I didn't particularly like, so I worked hard at being what I thought everyone else would like.

When I was eventually exposed to and became accepting of the gospel, God had some work to do on my heart. Essentially, I had to come to Him in a broken state.

I had been saved into a conservative denominational church that never really mentioned the Holy Spirit, but did have a strong focus on the Word of God and disciplines of the faith. As a new Christian, I was all-in. I became an avid Bible student and zealous worker in the church. Then, in my early twenties, I grew aware of a calling to become a full-time minister.

As I considered the significance of that calling and the depth of my inner brokenness, I could not see how the two could be reconciled. My introversion and insecurity were proving to be a roadblock to fruitful ministry.

> *My introversion and insecurity were proving to be a roadblock to fruitful ministry*

My fractured remnants of a family had never been close, thus intimacy with God was not something I had naturally sought. I had replaced the completion that comes from relationships with the independence that comes from driven-ness.

I had not yet discovered that Christian life is all about the heart. I just knew there was something wrong or missing, and had become concerned at my lack.

In the midst of this, despite my bias towards isolation, God took the initiative to steadily draw me closer to Him. It came to a head one cloudy day, while in my car overlooking the ocean. Considering my plight, I cried out, "I give you all my life for this cause, but I can't do it without your help!"

I bowed my head, more in defeat than piety. Instantly however, my chin seemed to be raised by God Himself! To my surprise, my mouth opened of its own accord and I started speaking out a language I have never heard. My mind was racing one way, but my tongue in another.

I came to realise later that God had released in me the gift of languages Paul mentions in First Corinthians.[1] The trouble was, at that time I didn't actually believe in that gift.

Over the following weeks, however, as I learned to exercise my new prayer language, I experienced a tangible increase in both my closeness to God and my personal boldness. I felt less driven, and more called. What is more, I found that I was giving from an inner abundance rather than a need to do what is right.

The trigger for this change is crucial to note. By God's grace, I had a developing hunger to know Him more, despite

---

[1] 1 Corinthians 14:1-23

my isolationist tendency. But the trigger point was that moment of surrender where I admitted that I had to rely on God in every way if I was to fulfil the mission He had for me.

It was a surrender of faith, and – interestingly – faith became the very thing that grew.

I was still quite broken, but now I was broken with power! The gifts of the Spirit had been released within me, even though the fruit of the Spirit was yet to catch up.

A Restless Heart

My next life-altering breakthrough took a lot longer to arrive. I am sure I could have shortened that process quite significantly, but my absence of understanding in God's ways prolonged my experience. A few years after my previous faith-building breakthrough, I had become troubled by the fact that, even though I could recognise a calling on my life, I was still nowhere near ready for vocational ministry.

I sensed that God was leading me into a wilderness season – a journey where He invites us into a new experience of Him, but which sometimes includes cutting off facets of our previous lifestyle. In my case, that meant my intense commitment to church-work was about to come under review.

When God calls us out like this, He is usually the One that does the cutting off, since few of us will do it voluntarily. My problem was that I needed my church-work more than it needed me. My enthusiasm and skill-set had granted a degree of recognition and reward that I had not previously known, and which was not entirely healthy for my soul.

God will eventually find a way stop us working for Him if it is out of our own inner deficit. He wants us to work with Him, motivated by His love alone. My pastor at the time saw right through me and at that time declared, "God doesn't want all that you do for Him ... He wants you."

> **God doesn't want all that you do for Him ... He wants you**

Within days, the multiple opportunities that had been laid before me to enter full-time ministry closed. It wasn't my pastor's doing; he was as surprised as I was! It just seemed to "happen" for a number of inexplicable reasons.

I thought it would be a season of weeks, or perhaps a month or two. But it didn't end. After what became a few years of "wilderness living," I began trying to push my way out of that season. But the doors of ministry that had once always been open to me continued to be shut tight. In my heart, I felt like a wildcat locked in a cage. I had lots of energy and felt my time was being wasted.

All this was going on inside me despite the fact that I was by then running a medium-sized company, was up to my neck in volunteer service at church, and was loving every moment of life with my young family. I didn't say I had lots of spare time; I was just restless for more.

My frustration was actually a pointer to a much larger, unseen problem – pride. I was blind to it, as all pride's victims are. It often hides itself in our well-intentioned, empire-building ambitions that never bring satisfaction. It even cloaks itself in a drive for good causes, and can be stealthily fuelled by our silent competition to keep up with others. Make no mistake, however; pride is on God's hit-list of things to deal with. And deal with it He did.

As I was driving to the office one day, I clearly heard that word "pride" echo through the car. I thought God was telling me that someone I knew must have a pride problem!

> **Pride is on God's hit-list of things to deal with**

"I will keep an eye out for them, Lord!" I said.

The next Sunday, my pastor called me up on stage because he felt he had a Word from God for me. I was excited until I heard it. "God is going to break you so He can bring increase in your life!"

"What sort of encouraging word is that?" I thought. I was already seven years into my wilderness. Who wants to be broken even more? I was soon to realise that I was only halfway there. And then, within days, my world fell completely apart.

Over the span of a few months, my wife began suffering from serious signs of breakdown, the production facility of our company burned to the ground, I was sued by a disgruntled employee, two of my friends died, my brother passed away, and I was fired in a corporate restructure that I had designed!

This spike of severe circumstance was followed up by seven years of constant and debilitating trials.

That added up to fourteen years in the wilderness. Towards the end, I had stopped counting the years and the losses. I had also lost interest in my own achievements. Those things had ceased to matter. Like a wild horse being prepared for service, I had been broken. But now I was broken in the right places.

I was happy to be getting on with life, simply attending my local church. I had no ministry role or even interest in such things by then. I was simply content with my life as it was.

But God had other ideas.

The Key Moment

The young preacher finished his message one Sunday and invited people to the front for prayer. Suddenly, I became numb all over and felt like my hands were on fire. I stumbled to the front of this small, conservative church, not knowing what to do. A few young adults came to the front also, and all I could think to do was lay a hand on their shoulder.

As I did, one after the other were touched by God's powerful anointing, and went flying backwards to the floor, as if unconscious. Thankfully, there were people in the front row to catch them! I didn't know what was happening, and didn't really care – God was tangibly with me and I was at peace. That was all that mattered.

Eventually I sat back down, half expecting to be thrown out of the building. But then a small old woman hobbled up behind me and began to prophesy. "God has seen your humble heart and is going to raise you up!"

"I really don't care what He does with me," I said. "I just want to be with Him like this for the rest of my life."

That moment my real ministry was born ... even though I had served the Lord consistently for twenty years. The fourteen years in the wilderness had done its work to the point where I didn't see it as a wilderness anymore. I was just hungry to grow and be with God; there was no ambition or pride left. When I looked for it, all I noticed was the tangible absence of the weight of my own importance. I felt free for the first time.

I had passed a tipping point. My old nature had finally been broken and submitted to the greater influence of a life in the Spirit.[2] The catalytic factor for my transformation was not an instant; it was an attitude that had grown. It was

---

[2] Romans 8:13

humility – a preparedness to submit to the hand of God in all areas of life.

If my earlier experience in God had taken me from being driven to being called, then this one brought me from the mindset of a slave to that of a son. I will unpack this idea later in the book.

My next key moment took place just weeks later, and was probably a continuation of the one explained above, but it is just as vital to explain.

I had moved out of the corporate world, and was by then the owner of my own small company with a handful of staff. I had been enjoying the experience for some time, but I knew it was time to get big or get out. I had also begun developing young leaders in our church and the love for ministry was returning.

As I began to talk it through with my wife, we knew the next move was obvious. It was time to walk away from business and go into vocational ministry. There was no talk of reduced income or what the cost would be – we just had to do it. Within a week, I was on staff at our church and the sale of my business was underway. Just like that!

The door I couldn't force open for fourteen years was now flung open at my initial interest.

I mention this moment because of the significance of the process. Each of us has a calling on our life, and assignments to undertake along the way. But we aren't ready to do any of them as we should until we have grappled with the idea of working with God in His way.

I had, for a few weeks, been growing a hunger to "go" for God – to take His love and give it to others. Anywhere would have been fine, and any role a privilege as long as it was serving God and people. I was actually offering to take on the role of church garbage collector when I was given the role of pastor.

That specific hunger to go – matched with the catalysing spark of preparedness to sacrifice – had ignited a love for people that God did not want to hold back. He had held me back when my motives were tainted, but now the lights were all green.

> *The hunger to go had ignited a love for people that God did not want to hold back*

THE BIGGER PICTURE

Let me revise these three key moments because they reflect the three key transitions in our spiritual maturity.

First there was a moment of deep reliance – of surrender to His ways. That catalyzed a rapid growth in faith.

Then, after many years, I had submitted the drives of my old nature to Christ. That was a gradual transition from being carnal to being spiritual – or empowered by the Holy

Spirit within – which Paul describes in First Corinthians chapter three.

Once I was empowered by the fruit of God's Spirit, and not my own ambition, I was then released in love.

The movements were initiated by three separate elements: a desire to know God, a desire to grow more like God, and a desire to go in God. These are the hungers that initiate change – and they become the fuel for the three rhythms of grace that I explain more fully in this book. What we will see is that God actually released faith, then hope, then love. These are the only things that matter and the only things that last.

Once you have those three things, you have everything.

Your Response:

Are you able to identify any key moments of spiritual transition in your life? Choose one of significance and make a note of the following:

What were the factors that brought you to the point of transition?

What were the evidences of transformation?

[1.4]

Walking with God

YOUR DEVELOPING LIFE STORY is a complex and organic journey. It is deeply personal. Much of it remains between you and God, as it should.

In the mire of that complexity, it can be hard to fathom His greater plan for you. Only God knows the end from the beginning, so He alone has the unique perspective of seeing your life as if looking back from the finish line. What looks to you as being confused, inconsistent in direction, and frustratingly slow, is from God's perspective a developing mosaic of grace and purpose.

Think for a moment on the seasons of growth and challenge that have come before you. What was God growing in you through that? Was it patience, forgiveness, endurance, or perhaps trust? The majority of what God builds in us is internal. He is concerned with and committed to growing our heart.

> **God is committed to growing our heart**

I let you in a few of my stories in the last chapter. You may or may not have related to any of the lessons, but what you will relate to are the moments of surrender and submission. You have had them too. They are like radical forks in the road where one path goes around the mountain while the other looks like it heads off a cliff.

Sooner or later, the idea of going around the mountain again is unacceptable, and you know it is time to leap in faith.

What may surprise you is the amount of consistency and intentionality there is in what God is doing in you and everyone else. Our paths all look radically different, and yet there are some flexible patterns and principles of redemption at work in all of us, which have been in place since we left the Garden of Eden.

THE BIG THREE

God is all about bringing you to life. Abundant life – a life full of peace and impact.[1] We are all called to experience that, although not all who are called by God choose to accept His offer or continue in the process.[2] As messy as the journey can

---

[1] John 10:10; John 15:16
[2] Matthew 22:14

be, if we are aware of what the big picture and process is, we can cooperate with it more easily.

Think again about what God has been developing in you. There are all sorts of specifics that relate to you alone, but if you could categorise what He is up to, it would help make sense of it all.

I like to reflect on the musings of the Apostle Paul on this. Now and again, he would break from his heavy theology and discussion of how we should be behaving, and reflect on issues of the heart. First Corinthians Chapter 13 is such a passage. There he is focussing on the eternal value of love in comparison to so much else that we busy ourselves with.

He declares that most of the very best we do in life is limited and temporal. But one day it will all be different. Then he gives the clincher: "And now these three remain: faith, hope, and love. But the greatest of these is love."[3]

Paul is saying that the only things in common between our life now and our life then will be those three things – faith, hope, and love.

When God is at work in you, He is building into you an eternal purpose that will never fade. He is developing only that which matters forever. We invest time and effort in building skills and possessions, all of which will disappear! God, however, builds your heart, and your heart lives on.

---

[3] 1 Corinthians 13:13

> **All that He is doing in you could be distilled down to these core elements: faith, hope, and love.**

All that He is doing in you could be distilled down to these core elements: faith, hope, and love.

He builds faith because our fallen bias is to be self-reliant and self-determined. While that can keep our minds busy, it ensures our hearts remain weary and alone. Our heart was made to dwell with and rely on Him, and God is determined to bring your heart home.

He restores hope because that is the very perspective of heaven. Hope is a way of thinking that has optimism based on the goodness and plans of God. Without hope, our hearts wither and fail. We are designed to be inspired by what is possible in Him.

God builds love because we are His children who reflect His image. God is love, it is His very nature. Therefore, He cannot help but sacrificially love. At our deepest level, we are at our best when we engage in that love, and in turn release it to a thirsty world.

The Developmental Journey

God's Spirit is constantly working to build faith, hope, and love within you. In your journey, though, you will be able to pinpoint moments where one facet in particular is being drawn out. With a little bit of awareness of your

Overview of the spiritual developmental journey

overall developmental journey, you can actually buy-in more intentionally to the process.

Although God is everywhere and knows everything, from a spiritual empowerment perspective we all start life spiritually disconnected from God. Until we are indwelt by His Spirit at the moment of our conversion, we are what scripture defines as "natural."[4] It means we are dust, doing it alone and obligated to follow our fallen nature.

Once we place our faith in Christ to save us by paying the price for sin that we could never pay, He comes in via the Holy Spirit. He is then our Emmanuel, "God with us," stamping His ownership on us as His children.[5] The Spirit's work in us does not commence when we place our faith in Him. Prior to salvation, He is calling, drawing, and at specific times even revealing the goodness of God to those who are still unconvinced. Even in our disconnected state, God takes the initiative to build a bridge into our hearts.

The movement out of this natural phase is significant. It is a movement emphasised by faith. The Spirit is in particular

---

[4] 1 Corinthians 2:14 (Greek: *psuchikos*)
[5] 2 Corinthians 1:22

focussing on spawning and then growing a foundational belief in God that is based on His existence, goodness, and truth.

Of course, once we have been born again the presence of the Spirit in our lives is no guarantee that we will always follow His lead. As you will realise, there are plenty of believers who reflect very little the fruit of the Spirit. Those of us in this early stage of development are defined by Paul as carnal.[6] It's an unfortunate term implying that our hearts are not empowered yet by God's Spirit. We are saved and going to heaven, but at best we live for God rather than from God.

This is not a stage we can bypass; we all start there. But God makes immediately available a pathway into the next stage of growth, which is simply called "spiritual."[7] Paul speaks in black-and-white terms in describing these two stages, yet in reality the transition between the two can be quite lengthy, as you saw in my own example in the previous chapter.

To be spiritual simply means that the old nature is not the driving force in our life. As Paul says in Romans 8:12, we no longer have an obligation to follow our carnal nature anymore; our only obligation is to become empowered by the Spirit.

---

[6] 1 Corinthians 3:1
[7] 1 Corinthians 3:1

Could we ever be regarded as fully spiritual? I don't think so. But we do reach significant points of maturity when specific parts of our old life are put to death and the Spirit of God empowers a more life-giving choice. Some have said that to be spiritual means that sin is now the exception rather than the rule.

As you are probably aware by now, making a choice to be Spirit-empowered is not as simple as it appears. The internal drivers in our life such as fear, lust, pride, anger, and judgment are fuelled by dysfunction and wounding. These take time to identify and deal with. Sadly, some people never grow out of this phase.

Christians who don't understand the process frequently lose hope. They get stuck in the identity of Romans Chapter 7 – a person who knows what they should do but remains a slave to the old nature. Yet this is not the description of a saved person; Paul is talking there in past tense. He is saying that he used to be like that, but now in Christ he has been set free.

> *You have permission to gain your identity from Romans 8, where we are free to follow the Spirit*

You have permission to gain your identity from Romans Chapter 8, where we are free to follow the Spirit. There we are described as sons, not slaves.

The personal transition between Romans 7 and 8 is sometimes a tough one, yet if we persevere, it always ends in freedom. Those who sow in tears will reap in joy.[8] God replaces a sense of fatalistic hopelessness with a new and profound hope. Once we see from His perspective, and enjoy a degree of ongoing freedom, we can begin to see a preferred future in Christ.

The actual process of change here comes from a combination of growing intimacy with God, and of behavioural change. These two elements work together symbiotically, both reliant on the other. When you dwell closer with Christ, you can't help but be empowered by His presence; when you make choices to follow His ways, His Spirit empowers that same choice, making it possible.

In regard to the next movement, that of going, you saw from my experience that it happened relatively quickly. Paul didn't define this next stage, perhaps because he simply assumed it was an inevitable outworking of being a spiritual person.

Once we genuinely pass the tipping point where we are embracing the fullness of God's Spirit, the overflow of that grace is indeed inevitable. The first movement emphasises faith, the second brings hope, but this third movement is all about love – the greatest of all.

---

[8] Psalm 126:5

It is the stage of maturity where you give of what you have received. This is where a true abundance of spiritual fruit is seen. In some ways, you just can't help it!

However, so many try with good intentions to live this way before their time. They try to give from what they have not yet received and inevitably become dry from the over-reach. We are indeed able and expected to bear real fruit in every season of our journey, but it is this last one where we see an exponential increase in kingdom effectiveness.

Walking it Out

Walking with God refers to a state of the heart, not a physical activity (although for some it helps to literally go for a walk)!

Ultimately, our priorities, actions, and lifestyle are determined by the state of our inner world. That which is within will always determine how we behave on the outside. You can't bring peace to the world if you have only chaos in your heart. You can't give grace if you don't know how to embrace it yourself. But when your heart is full of the presence and fruit of the Holy Spirit, you simply can't help but change the world.

> *Ultimately, our priorities, actions, and lifestyle are determined by the state of our inner world*

When Peter and John came across the lame man in Acts 3, they were acutely aware of what they did and didn't have.

The man asked for money, but they gave a better solution ... Jesus. It wasn't a theory – they didn't merely believe certain things about Jesus. They carried Him with them.

"Silver and gold we don't have, but such as we have we give to you. Rise up and walk."[9]

Each of the stages and movements I have outlined describe a state of our heart as it discovers new depth in engagement with God. The rhythms of grace I will unwrap in the coming chapters are specific types of cooperative interaction with God. Through each movement, a different rhythm comes to the fore. All of them, however, follow the primary tempo of walking and working with God – of God doing His work and us doing ours.

Take a moment now to come before God and ask, "What is it you are doing in me? Where do you want me to grow?"

Why not write down what you think the answer might be. It will help you to apply some of the principles that come later in this book.

Your Response:

What is God actually developing in you in this season? Is it a specific fruit of the Spirit, or might it be a specific form of surrender or submission to His will? Write down your thoughts and include any of the circumstances which have contributed to this issue coming to the fore.

---

[9] Acts 3:6

[1.5]

Working with God

WE HAVE TALKED A lot so far about your inner walk with God, and how your level of engaged intimacy with Him will determine the fruitfulness of your life. Now we look at the fruitfulness itself, a topic best covered after that discussion on the inner core.

We as human beings will always be driven to do and create things, whether that is a family, a career, or a project. It is possible to do things with or without a good motive, and with or without God's obvious help. It is the way we are wired. However, if the form and function of our inner core is not set right, our labour will be fruitless from a kingdom viewpoint.

When Jesus said that without Him, we could do nothing, He was relating it to bearing fruit for God.[1]

---

[1] John 15:1-5

You can do lots of things without God's help! You can choose a life of sin and selfishness; you can burn up your own strength in activities that aren't God's will; you can even set all sorts of godly-looking goals. But they will bear no lasting fruit unless you are in partnership with Jesus, combining your dust with His breath.

The only way to have a fruitful life is to do God's will God's way. Listen again to Jesus' heart and method:

> Are you tired? Worn out? Burned out on religion? Come to me. Get away with me and you'll recover your life. I'll show you how to take a real rest. Walk with me and work with me—watch how I do it. Learn the unforced rhythms of grace. (Matthew 11:28-29 MSG)

> *If either walking or working are held in isolation, your fruitfulness will end*

You cannot work for God as you should unless you can first walk with God – and walking with God as you should will always compel you to get to work! If either walking or working are held in isolation, your fruitfulness will end.

Incessant walkers can become enamoured with introversion. They inevitably get stuck in their growth because the river of God's power simply must have an outlet, otherwise the bearer becomes stale.

Obsessive workers will by necessity be running on their own strength and limitations. They too often do work without bearing fruit. They become frustrated and stale as they wonder why God or His people don't seem to back their cause.

It is better to throttle back any obsession for either walking or working, and intentionally settle in to the even pace Jesus promotes.

Working in Partnership

The idea of restful work sounds like a paradox. How do you exert effort and not become drained by it? In truth, you do still become drained, but only to the extent that you have been required to contribute.

> **God never calls us to do nothing, nor will He call us to do anything without His help**

In other words, God's strength is always involved in bearing His fruit, but so is a degree of yours. You are a co-worker, so when you are fulfilling His calling or assignment, you are also playing your part.

Jesus said that without Him we could do nothing. But that wasn't permission for us to stand back and watch! God never calls us to do nothing, nor will He call us to do anything without His help. Paul explained this dynamic in Colossians 1:29, saying, "To this end I strenuously contend with all the energy Christ so powerfully works in me."

Having experienced seasons where I have done well at this partnership, and seasons where I have not done so well, I have come to recognise the difference more readily. The evidence of God's involvement in our efforts is that there is always fruit that could only come from His hand. Further, the effort expended by me in that process is far less than if I had attempted the same work alone. And the actual fruit that results is quite supernatural in itself.

MADE TO DO

When we walk closely with God in faith, hope, and love – the abundance flows from the inside out. Our heart naturally longs for the world to experience what we have.

Or at least it should. The reality can be somewhat more complicated. Our fears, our brokenness, our latent family and church culture, or our introversion can conspire to keep our eyes focussed inward.

Walking with God is addictive – the peace and joy we find in His presence will always leave us hungering for more. However, that desire to remain quietly in His presence can become the very throttle to experiencing Him fully.

Allow me to illustrate. Very occasionally I have been invited by friends to try out their new sports car. I grew up around race tracks and learned to drive at racing speeds before I had a road license so I appreciate a vehicle with those capacities.

Sports cars look and feel incredible! Some owners sit gazing at their machine for hours; a few even have pictures of them on their office wall. When I sit in a thoroughbred car that is obviously built for high speeds, however, I get a little frustrated. The leather seats are nice and the electronics are impressive, but I don't want to drive it on the public road; it would almost seem a waste. To dawdle around in traffic with people admiring from a distance is not for me. I want to get on a racing track and drive the car to fulfil its design. I want to test the limits, race against others, and enjoy being close to the edge.

But that's just me ... or is it?

God's plan for us is that we grow and bear fruit. The process for this is called sanctification. Before that word became identified with the Judeo-Christian faith, it meant to "restore or set apart to fulfil the original design." It essentially still means that. God works in us to make us holy and conformed to His image, because that is what we were created for in the first place.

> *Unless we are fulfilling our design, we are going to grow stale and our potential will be wasted!*

In a sense, we are like that sports car. Unless we are fulfilling our design, we are going to grow stale and our potential will be wasted!

We are designed to not only be. Our being is made for doing.

Green Light

When Jesus sent out seventy-two followers for their first mission experiment, I am sure they would have been a little nervous. The job profile started with Jesus describing them as sheep among wolves; their performance indicator was to heal the sick. The whole mission was impossible in their own strength, as is everything God calls us to do.

But on their return, their excitement held no bounds. They exchanged war stories and enjoyed the comradery that only brothers-in-arms can know. Trepidation had been converted to celebration.

> *Our stagnation may come from the fact that there is more than one green light put before us.*

Jesus had given His followers a green light to go, and it hasn't changed colour to this day. However, that leads us to the most common of believers' questions: "Where am I to go in Jesus' name?"

Our common confusion, and our subsequent stagnation, comes from the fact that there is more than one green light put before us. We may have been taught that to go means we head to another culture and evangelise the local unreached people. That is an option, but it is not the only option.

What if we have a young family and sense God's call to raise them in a close community of friends where they are? That would certainly make going to the mission field a hard option to consider. Our green light seems to be heading in a different direction.

The final chapters of this material will cover this concept further, but in short, God has given us several green lights in scripture that we have permission to pursue. They broaden the concept of mission as we begin to realise that our overarching purpose is to commune with God and extend His reign. Understanding these green lights will give you permission to be fruitful in every season of life while also being free to be you.

Assignments and Calling

As we progress through life, we inevitably grow as each season presents new challenges and opportunities. With each season comes specific assignments from God, each with varying duration.

While these assignments to work with Him are part of your calling, they are not in themselves your calling. Some of them may even seem to shoot off in a direction that counters who you believe God has called you to be. But don't worry, they are specific tasks that both utilise your current capacity in Him, and also equip you in ways your own logic would not have considered.

One of my early assignments was to pioneer a business start-up. My heart was for serving God, but His leading and open door into this experience had been clear. In those few short years I learned a broad set of skills in dealing with people, understanding finance and law, self-management, and even sales. I was given a fast-track in how to form an organisation, which was to become indispensable in later seasons of ministry and life.

Some assignments exist to impact a certain place or group of people. Others, like the one just described, take you into a specific vocational season.

Assignments from God are usually more easily defined than calling is; they often give clarity on what is to be done in the medium term. They give us the joy of making plans and setting goals. When Jesus sent out the seventy-two in pairs, it was an assignment. It had a beginning and an end, and clear outcomes were achieved.

> *Excitement and progress thrive on intentionality!*

Assignments provide a sense of intentionality about what we do. Excitement and progress thrive on intentionality! It is the way God wired us.

Assignments are like roads drawn on the landscape of your calling in Christ. The calling itself is less precise. It can encompass your various assignments, and indeed they serve to progress that calling. But calling is a much grander concept. Your calling can seem to be a place that always appears over the next horizon. That's because your calling is not what you do; it is who you are becoming.

In scriptural terms, your calling is your name. What you do is a product of who you are right now. What you will do is a product of who you are becoming.

Some have described calling as your true north. It is a direction to take rather than a task you can define.

God is leading you through the landscape of life in the general direction of your true north. However, if you try to over-define your calling in terms of the assignments He has given, you might struggle. God intends to do in you more than you can ask or imagine; therefore, unlike assignments, your calling is not a clear goal to be achieved. To do so would only limit what God does.

He simply wants you to become more of who you are – stripped of the baggage of the old nature and thriving ever more in the grace of God. You are only who you truly are when you are found closely engaged with God – living from the radical core of faith, hope, and love. That is your true north.

> *You are only who you truly are when you are found closely engaged with God*

For the next three weeks, we will delve much closer into each of these core elements. Each has a wonderful rhythm of grace of its own. They synchronise beautifully, and combine to create the fruitful lifestyle of walking and working with God.

Your Response:

What assignment has God got you on right now? In what ways do you need His strength to be fruitful in that work?

[2.1]

Faith Foundations

WHAT DOES IT MEAN to you to have faith?

My unbelieving friends describe it somewhat differently from the way I do. They believe that faith is blind, that it is a leap in the dark. They see faith as something that stands in opposition to reason – a belief in something that has no proof.

I enjoy giving them testimony of the undeniable things I have seen God do in my life and that of others – things that prove God exists. Faith is far from blind or unreasonable. Indeed, it is the only thing that makes sense.

Yet it is easy for us Christians to also form a slightly skewed view of faith. We may limit faith to mean that we believe in God to change our circumstance or save us in some way from the troubles of this broken world. He does do that, of course. Incredibly so at times! And, as mentioned, it forms a great testimony to the reality of God.

But when we say we have faith in Jesus, what exactly should that mean?

> **Faith is not merely a cognitive belief; it results in us actively leaning on what we believe**

The words "faith" and "belief" are rooted in the same Greek word: *pistis*. It means to rely on something. It is an active word, not a passive one. Faith is not merely a cognitive belief; it is a belief that results in us actively leaning on – or depending on – what we believe.

To believe in Jesus does not mean we merely agree that He exists; it means that we rely on the price He paid for our sin rather than on our own ability to earn right standing with God. We don't believe Jesus died for our sin ... and then also try to ensure we are good with God by performing at some level.

The action component of faith is to rely on Jesus' death completely and not have a Plan B. This definition of faith means that believing in that which is uncertain is not really faith. It might be better described as hope.

In Jesus' day, people began to believe in Him mainly because He demonstrated who He was. Yet Jesus sometimes became frustrated at the limited faith of those people. In John 4:48 He rebuked them, saying, "Unless you people see signs and wonders you will never believe." He was hoping for more, looking for those who believed in spite of what they saw.

"Blessed are those who have not seen and yet have believed," He said after His resurrection.[1] What was Jesus getting at there? It's not that He was expecting people to believe in what they didn't know. Rather, He was expecting that what they knew would get them through anything they were to see.

He longed for a level of faith that didn't fail when things went badly – a faith that overcame any circumstance, rather than needing the circumstance to change.

God is looking for faith through any circumstance, more than faith for any circumstance.

> ***God is looking for faith** through any circumstance, more than **faith** for any circumstance*

Facets of Faith

What are we to have faith in? What can we know that will compel us to act a biblical way?

Before all else, we obviously need to believe that God exists. This is the simplest and smallest type of faith because there is obviously so much evidence to prove the fact. The

---

[1] John 20:29

testimony of creation, the mountain of undeniably changed hearts, the historical proof of the resurrection and countless miracles, and even the consistent cry of the human heart for a sense of eternity and meaning – these all make faith in God's existence easy for those who genuinely seek truth.

Beyond belief in God's existence, we can have faith in His goodness of character as well. First John 4:16 states that we can know and rely on the love God has for us because God is love. God cannot be evil; there is no mischief or darkness in Him. Love is His very nature, and all He does comes from the goodness of that love.

> *Our relationship with God should not be confined to the words of the book He authored*

We can also have faith in God's Word. God is without fault, therefore His Word is always true. God's Word is found in scripture, and also in His Word spoken to you. God always has more to say – He has promises, ideas, and direction for you every moment of the day. Jesus only said what He heard His Father saying, and He only did what His Father was doing.

This may sound provocative, but our relationship with God should not be confined to the words of the book He authored. We don't have a relationship with a load of paper, but with the living words that dwell within them. These living words come from the living Word, who is alive today. You can be sure that what He speaks to your heart will never be in contradiction to what is found in scripture. Indeed, if you want to know what God is saying, dwell on what you know He has already said – the Bible. Then listen to the direct whispers of God as He guides you in that context.

Romans 10:17 says, "Faith comes through hearing, and hearing by the word of God." In that context, Paul is talking about the preaching of the gospel – the spoken word about Christ. So you can see that the Word of God can be heard by us in a number of ways. But they should all build our faith and be in line with what He has previously said.

Next, we also exercise unyielding faith in the atoning work of Christ for our salvation. His sacrifice was complete, not needing to be redone every time we routinely fall short. God's wrath has already been totally removed for those who trust in Jesus' death for their sin.[2]

The final component of this foundational faith is a reliance on the total sufficiency of God. He alone is always enough. We do not need God to alter circumstance in our favour in order for our spirit to thrive. He meets every valid need. As God said clearly to Paul, who had prayed for healing in his body, "My grace is sufficient for you."[3] This is the faith that gets the applause of heaven, and this is the faith Jesus sought the most in His followers.

---

[2] 1 John 2:2; Hebrews 9:12
[3] 2 Corinthians 12:9

When it comes to the three eternal elements of our heart (faith, hope, and love), faith is the proverbial currency of heaven. Those in scripture who had great faith are not only applauded, but they are also frequently rewarded.

Jesus Himself often declared that a person's faith had made them well.[4] And Paul's clear theology is that we are saved by grace through faith.[5] Even though it is God's grace that does the work, it is accessed by us through faith.

And whilst he clearly stated that the greatest of the three core elements is love, Paul also said that our righteousness before God comes through faith from first to last.[6] Even though love – both for God and from God – is primary above all things, it is faith in God that counters the humanistic bias to rely on self, which is so destructive to our engagement with God.

Faith for More

Having laid the foundational elements of faith, we have permission to build a valid "mustard seed" faith that can move mountains.

God is still very much in the business of invading our world in overt and powerful ways. We are expected to have

---

[4] Matthew 9:22; Mark 5:34, 10:52; Luke 7:50; Luke 18:42
[5] Ephesians 2:8
[6] Romans 1:17

faith in Him to do that, so long as it is built on the solid foundation mentioned above.

The faith we need in operating in the spiritual gifts, for seeing the miraculous, or for any other spiritual intervention in our world is best derived from hearing and releasing God's Word. Jesus confined His works to precisely that – following the Father's guidance. The New Testament particularly is packed with examples of God breaking through in amazing ways. There is no sensible argument to make us infer that He has stopped working in our lives.

The truth is, all those amazing events from scripture – and more – are happening right now in every culture globally, including the west. They can be expected by the empowered Christian when our radical core truly gets radical.

Before we look at how to start a journey towards this, let's look at how Jesus Himself mentored the disciples in their fledgling faith. The twelve didn't simply switch on unlimited belief when Jesus granted them authority to work in His name. Matthew 28:17 reminds us that even though they had witnessed incredible things, including Jesus' resurrection, they continued to doubt. They underwent a prolonged growth journey that was ultimately

> *Even though they had witnessed incredible things, ... they continued to doubt*

and significantly impacted by the events described in the second chapter of Acts and the coming of the Holy Spirit.

Step back a year or two, however, when they were still in their early training with Jesus, and the journey of growing faith is more obviously seen. Mark Chapter 9 gives us a clear snapshot of the challenges faced by these very normal people as they attempted to apply faith in a way that made a difference to life. You may remember the story, but I will summarise it here.

It takes place the day after Jesus, Peter, James, and John had encountered Moses and Elijah on the Mount of transfiguration. As they returned, the other nine disciples were up to their neck in disappointment, doubt, and debate with the angry locals because they had not been able to deliver a young boy of a demon. The distraught father came directly to Jesus to explain the situation.

The interesting thing to note here is that these same disciples had been authorised to cast out demons a few chapters earlier in Mark's gospel, and had seen success. Experience and authority were not the issue.

Jesus' response is telling, to both the crowd and the disciples. He highlights a lack of faith as the issue, declaring in Mark 9:19 that they are an unbelieving generation. The father of the boy then gives voice to the same desire we all harbour ... "I believe, help me overcome my unbelief!"

Jesus proceeds to cast the demon out of the boy, but later the disciples asked Him privately about the reasons behind their own failure to cast it out. Jesus responds by saying that prayer and fasting held the key (v. 29).

Reading this with formulaic eyes, some have concluded that prayer and fasting must activate a form of "cause-and-effect" response from God. The implication is, "If we do this, then God is somehow obliged to do that." So they submit themselves to rigorous disciplines and practices in an effort to increase results.

But take a closer look at the story. Lack of faith was the real problem, not the power of a demon. Prayer was the solution to that lack of faith. Prayer and fasting were suggested by Jesus as mechanisms for the disciples to engage more closely and intuitively with God Himself, not as a way to incite Him to act. The principle at play here is that time spent in the presence of the Faithful One will always result in an increase of faith!

> *Time spent in the presence of the Faithful One will always result in an increase of faith!*

Jesus, of course, had already built intimacy with God through a deep well of constant fellowship, so He merely had to administer the authority that came from that.

As with every kingdom principle you will find in this material, the answer to our fruitlessness, restlessness, and dryness of soul is found in engaging intimately with God Himself.

In the next session, we will look a little deeper at the specific rhythm of grace that can be so helpful in growing faith. But we leave this session focussed on the fact that God calls us into a relationship that is personal, not merely functional. He wants to engage with us much more than He wants to see us perform things for Him. He longs for us to desire Him more than we desire progress or achievement.

All that we do should flow from this place of abundant love and grace.

Your Response:

In what area of your life do you most strongly rely on God? How does that faith make you differ from those around you that have no faith? Are your choices and priorities different? How does your faith direct your life?

[2.2]

Spirit and Truth

FAITH, THE FIRST OF the three core elements that God is growing within each of us who are called by His name, is active reliance on God. Everything about the Christian worldview and practice is built on the fundamental premise of this thing called faith. Faith is not merely believing in something you cannot see or prove. It is relying on something or someone in a way that goes beyond mere theory or hope.

Faith has a substantive element to it in that it is not complete unless we actually lean on our belief in some way. For example, when I go to sit on a wooden chair, I first assess and hope that it can hold my weight. If I believe it to the point that I actually sit on the chair, then I am exhibiting my faith in it. By the same token, when I examine the gospel message, I might cognitively agree that Jesus died for my sins, but until I place my salvation and eternity in His hands unreservedly, I have not exercised faith.

Hebrews 11:1 says that faith is the substance of things hoped for. We act on what we believe, and so James 2:18 can rightly say, "I will show you my faith by my deeds."

Have you ever wondered how your faith levels are going?

In our last session, we saw a man who exhibited a great deal of candour before Jesus saying, "I believe, help me overcome my unbelief" (Mark 9:24). He, like most of us, probably didn't realise he needed more faith until his current level was put to the test.

> ***God will constantly be presenting us with situations that require us to adopt a new level of faith***

We normally build our lifestyle, career, ministries, and spiritual expression around the level of faith we currently have. We seldom consciously stretch our faith – either because we don't realise we should or we just don't know how.

God, however, will constantly be presenting us with situations that require us to adopt a new level of faith. He knows that the faith we had yesterday won't cope with tomorrow's situations, so He continually seeks to grow the faith that is in us.

Growing Faith

The Apostle Paul, with his legal mind, clinically summed up the process God uses to build faith in Romans 10:17: "Faith comes from hearing the message, and the message is heard through the word about Christ."

There are two elements here: the word itself, and our hearing of the word. For us to hear in a biblical sense, it takes more than listening. We must understand, process, and apply that word which we ultimately come to believe is true. But we also need God to reveal truth. We cannot constrain truth to the limits of our human capacity.

Jesus said that no one comes to the Father lest He draw Him, thus there is an inescapable spiritual component at play in this digesting of truth.[1] Spirit and Truth combine to become a catalyst for faith.

Let's see how Jesus applied this at ground level. In the fourth chapter of John, we read about the encounter Jesus had with a Samaritan woman who was drawing water from the local well.

She had a degree of faith already. She acknowledged God and knew the basics about the Messiah who was coming, yet her lifestyle was disconnected from the ramifications of that. Her numerous marriages had ended and her life was defined as a failure by those of her community. She showed hope in God, but no personal faith in Him.

---

[1] John 6:44

As Jesus zeroed in on the woman's heart, she threw out a distractive argument, saying that to worship God, one had to go to the temple in Jerusalem. In John 4:24, Jesus countered her side-track with a principle, the ramifications of which go wider than a surface reading would present. He said, "God is Spirit, and His worshippers must worship in Spirit and in truth."

This couplet of Spirit and Truth that Jesus used came off the tongue so naturally we might assume He had used it before, or certainly thought it through.

We know that to please God or even come to Him, we must have faith. Hebrews 11:6 says that "without faith it is impossible to please God," yet Jesus says that the worshippers God seeks are those who worship in Spirit and Truth.

> ***Jesus is giving us a mechanism that leads to faith through engaging God***

Could it be that, as with the disciples who lacked the faith to deliver the boy in the previous session, Jesus is giving us a mechanism that leads to faith through engaging God? In yesterday's session, Jesus recommended prayer and fasting, but in this case He is suggesting worship that is based in Spirit and truth.

In both cases, He is pointing people directly to the face of God as the answer to their lack of faith. He knows that time spent in the shadow of the Faithful One will always grow our faith.

But what was Jesus getting at by using the term Spirit and Truth with the Samaritan woman? Unlike the disciples, she had held up a belief-blocker in the form of religious rules that the Jews had imposed, which inhibited where she could worship even if she had wanted to. She was believing a lie about God, and Jesus was setting her straight with truth. His point was that you can worship God anywhere and anytime because God is Spirit and we come to Him at that level. If you are to worship Him, do it based on who He really is, and who you really are. Come to Him spirit-to-Spirit.

Jesus used this little couplet of Spirit and Truth to remove the woman's barrier to God and to give her access to faith, but there is so much more to be found in living by Spirit and Truth.

What God has joined, let no man separate

As a pastor, I spend a lot of my time in the church world surrounded by Christian believers. As with any voluntary gathering of people, like attracts like. People of common belief and culture tend to like each other's company. We have groups, churches, and even whole denominations created around similarity rather than diversity.

One of the more natural, sociological polarities we form is our preference for either a thoughtful, word-centred culture or an expressive and emotive, Spirit-centred culture. Because of our personal preference, we gravitate to one side or the other of a perceived line in the sand, and potentially justify it from scripture or anecdotes of the "errors" of the other side.

> **We divide what Jesus had put together – Spirit and Truth – as if they are combatants**

In essence, we divide what Jesus had put together – Spirit and Truth – as if they are combatants, or at best opposites. Yet they are not; they are complimentary and dependent on the other to find their fullness. To separate them robs each of their full potential. I have fellowshipped at both word-centred and Spirit-centred churches, and for all their strengths, they both inevitably lack what the other brings.

As Jesus repeatedly said, "the Spirit leads us in to all truth,"[2] and the truth about God will always point us directly into His presence. Look for example at this simplest of illustrations of the Samaritan woman coming to a saving faith in Christ. Jesus got her attention initially by listening to the Spirit and sharing knowledge about her previous relationships, information that He could never have naturally known. Then He debunks with truth the myth she held about localised worship.

With this one-two combination of Spirit and Truth, her final barriers to salvation evaporated. Spirit and Truth definitely built faith in her case.

---

[2] John 14:17; 15:26; 16:13

But what about her own inner experience of salvation? The Spirit of God was at work in her inner world, convicting of sin and revealing the Father. As she had her rational arguments removed, she saw and believed the truth: Jesus was the Messiah she was hoping for. Spirit and Truth combined to release saving faith.

The Apostle Paul was the all-star poster child for Spirit and Truth, in particular with evangelism. He preached the word zealously, and demonstrated the gospel with Spirit-empowered signs and wonders. In Romans 15:18-19 he said of his own ministry, "I will not venture to speak of anything except what Christ has accomplished through me in leading the Gentiles to obey God by what I have said and done—by the power of signs and wonders, through the power of the Spirit of God. So from Jerusalem all the way around to Illyricum, I have fully proclaimed the gospel of Christ."

Did you get that? The gospel was only fully proclaimed when both word and (Spirit-empowered) deeds were seen – in other words, Spirit and Truth.

Engaging in God's Rhythm

Before we delve even deeper in the next session into the dynamic of Spirit and Truth, let us recap how the rhythms of grace apply here, and why the symbiosis of two apparently contradictory elements is so powerful.

The fundamental principle at play in the rhythms is that God partners with us in fulfilling His plan for us to have fruitful lives. He predominantly works with us, not for us, since we are meant to be co-workers and friends with Him.

Having God working with us means that He has His part to play, and we have ours. God's grace gives us what we can't give ourselves, and yet He works with willing partners who seek Him and make room for Him. The rhythms of grace are the demonstration of this dynamic where each role is fulfilled in partnership, and we enjoy a life of fruitful rest.

With this specific rhythm of Spirit and Truth, God Himself meets us on a spiritual level, revealing Himself, encouraging and saving us. We must come into alignment with Him by searching out and believing the truth about who God really is. By combining these two elements, we can't help but grow in faith.

> *There is a time to press forward and a time to lean back.*

You may also notice that in each of the rhythms of grace, there is also an element of rest. There is a time to press forward and a time to lean back.

Sabbath rest is a major point of the whole thing. Remember Jesus words in Matthew 11:28 MSG: "I'll show you how to take a real rest. Walk with me and work with me—watch how I do it. Learn the unforced rhythms of grace."

The Rest of Faith

The essence of faith is to rely on God and not ourselves. It is a life that is not forced, nor reliant on our own strength. As we look at the interaction between Spirit and Truth, we can see that our part is to look for truth about the nature and goodness of God, and believe it. That might not seem to be a great deal of work, yet many struggle to do it.

The Pharisees knew every part of the Old Testament Law, which was the sum total of truth as they knew it at the time, yet they still relied on their own self-righteous work to earn favour with God. They quizzed Jesus, saying, "What must we do to do the works God requires?"

Jesus answered, "The work of God is this: to believe in the one He has sent."[3]

Pontius Pilate, a man entangled in the power and politics of his day, could not disengage from it long enough to look into Jesus' eyes and discover meaning and salvation. "What is truth?" he muttered while at the same moment turning His back on Jesus. His life was so complex, and his need for the rewards of position so strong he could not afford to hear the answer to his own question.

Will you pause long enough today from your own life to dwell on the truth of who Jesus is? Remember what He has done. Meditate on the ramifications of His eternal gift of

---

[3] John 6:28-29

salvation and grace and how it determines the meaning of your life. Does the work you invest in so heavily really matter?

Then, invite His Spirit to give you counsel. Ask Him to reveal more of the Father to you.

The Sabbath rest available to you is one of faith. Faith that God is enough for you, and enough to take care of the situation you find yourself in – whether it be relational, vocational, or internal.

Hebrews 4:9-10 says, "There remains, then, a Sabbath-rest for the people of God; for anyone who enters God's rest also rests from their works, just as God did from His."

Rest today in who God is, and what He is doing for you right now.

Your Response:

Our faith in God grows when we know the truth about who He is, and engage with Him through his powerful Holy Spirit. Romans 8:16 says that the Spirit Himself testifies with our spirit that we are children of God. In regard to Spirit & Truth, which of the two elements does your personality type more naturally embrace? What are some ways that you could develop the other facet of this rhythm of grace?

[2.3]
Faith to Walk

Faith for the In-between

It has been said that taking the first step of a journey is the hardest. When it comes to our journey of faith, such a statement may not be entirely accurate. For most of us, the first step is the easiest. We – like the Samaritan woman at the well – are confronted with the reality and power of Jesus, the need for a Saviour, and the availability of salvation. It becomes something of a no-brainer. Of course we take that first step!

Now begins the process of navigating life with all its seasonal challenges and joys, in the midst of the same circumstances that are common to all. Yet we do it with the massive advantage of having Jesus with us the whole way.

If we are honest with ourselves though, some days it doesn't really feel like an advantage. Sure, there are times when we are so aware of His greatness and His proximity and we can't help but smile, even wink at adversity. But in other seasons we struggle to engage or appreciate Him at all, let alone sense His strength in our veins.

This is life in-between.

We are in-between the salvation moment where "all things are made new,"[1] at least in a spiritual sense, and the salvation that will be perfect one day when body, soul, and spirit are with Jesus forever.

> **We need faith that finds rest in the midst of trouble, rather than require the trouble to go away.**

To navigate the in-between, we need a different expression of faith. We need faith that finds rest in the midst of trouble, rather than require the trouble to go away. We need faith that knows God is good and God is close, even when we can't sense Him and the world denies Him. We need faith to call on Him to act in power, and faith to work in the spiritual gifts He gives each of us.

This is where the power of God's rhythms of grace come in. Our inner engine room of faith can come to life, revived by the synergy of Spirit and Truth as they work together to wake up our spirit and sustain us.

---

[1] 2 Corinthians 5:17

God Himself has promised, "Even to your old age and grey hairs I am He, I am He who will sustain you. I have made you and I will carry you; I will sustain you and I will rescue you."[2]

Sustaining Faith

Christians start off easily believing God's promise that He will sustain us, but later we may trip over the reality that being sustained does not always equate being rescued from life's difficulties. In fact, Jesus was pretty clear when He said that trouble was coming, but that through Him we can overcome it all.[3]

It becomes obvious that His sustaining power is often internal, and not circumstantial. Sure, He can heal us, He can change circumstances for our benefit, He can and often does do incredible and obvious things in our midst ... but remember this: with maturing believers He works with us more than He works for us.

> **With maturing believers God works with us more than He works for us**

Let us analyse this concept in the life of the Apostle Paul. He endured suffering that would tempt anyone to seek a softer path, yet he lived for decades after his stunning

---

[2] Isaiah 46:4
[3] John 16:33

salvation experience with a sustaining faith that kept him white-hot for God.

He writes of one of his more difficult seasons where some physical infirmity was plaguing him. He described it as a messenger of Satan, an attack with a demonic agenda. As one who trusted in God as a higher power than anything Satan could thrust his way, Paul appealed to God to take the affliction away. God answered with an even more profound solution. He gave grace for Paul to overcome despite the circumstance, saying "My grace is sufficient for you, for my power is made perfect in weakness."[4]

Just prior to this, Paul had experienced incredible highs that might have incited pride, and he knew it. He understood that God was better glorified by His own power and grace shining through than Paul's, and his choice for humility positioned Paul to come into alignment with God's enabling grace through the pain.

> **We are not always positioned to receive that which is offered**

God's grace is always there for us; He never withholds, yet we are not always positioned to receive that which is offered. As with saving grace, it is available to all, but not automatic. We must cooperate with grace by adopting the posture to receive it.

---

[4] 2 Corinthians 7-10

This is how the rhythms of grace work, and why so many revert to doing life under their own horsepower. They assume that whatever is available from God is theirs automatically, and that all they have is all He has! However, being aware of the gap between what they have and what they need, they begin to doubt God and work from a humanistic, self-sufficient mindset. Inevitably, this sequence of choices leaves them tired and dissatisfied!

Agreeing with Truth

To embrace the work of the Spirit, we need to agree with His perspectives and align with Him rationally. We are required embrace His truth. Amos 3:3 asks, "Can two walk together, except they be agreed?" Have you ever tried running in a three-legged race? If so, you know how important it is to keep in step with your partner, else you fall over each other. This is why Paul also said that since we live by the Spirit, we must also keep in step with the Spirit.[5]

> *If we agree with lies about ourselves, our God, and our purpose, how can we ever perceive His truth?*

Our minds are the gateway to the world of faith. If we agree with lies about ourselves, our God, and our purpose, how can we ever perceive His truth? If our minds are convinced that

---

[5] Galatians 5:25

we are alone and discarded, how could we ever trust Him enough with our hearts to receive His care?

Paul had to keep his thinking clear. There were certain truths he needed to keep as bedrock to his soul. They included the beliefs he wrote about often:

- That God is able to meet all his needs.

- That God is inherently good – He doesn't withhold, He doesn't change His mood, and He always loves.

- That God alone is enough for every situation – meaning that our internal and external worlds are sustained by Him.

- That God's word is true – what He says He does, and there is no shadow of a lie in Him.

All of this is on the truth side of this rhythm of grace. They were Paul's responsibility to believe. But do you see how this works? Paul didn't have to actually do any work here; God was to do all of it.

> *Paul did have to believe the truth. That was his job and it is ours*

Paul did, however, have to believe the truth. That was his job and it is ours. When the Pharisees asked Jesus, "What is the work God requires?" Jesus replied that the work God requires of us is to believe.[6]

---
[6] John 6:28-29

It is hard to overstate the value of clear thinking in relation to our spiritual life. We are empowered by that kingdom with which we agree. It is as if we are a sailing boat that relies on wind to get anywhere, yet there are two opposing winds blowing at the same time. One is the wind of the Holy Spirit offering empowerment and grace to fulfil God's will. The other wind has satanic origins; it is always tempting us to engage with its lies, ready to draw us deep into isolation and sin.

> ***We are empowered by that kingdom with which we agree***

I have control over how I trim the sails on my boat. By choosing what I will believe and agree with, I can set the sails to receive God's wind. He empowers that choice and takes the boat where it cannot go on its own. Likewise, I can believe lies and let the evil realm take power over that choice to the point where it seems I was obliged to go that way all along. To choose wisely, it is vital to remember that, as Romans 8:12 says, we have no obligation at all to the old nature.

Spirit of Grace

When God replied to Paul's prayer for Him to remove the thorn, He said that His grace for Paul was sufficient. In our culture, "sufficient" is not a word that incites a hugely positive reaction. It reminds us of the minimum mark we need to pass a test; it is just enough. Is that what God gives, just enough to get by and no more? No, He doesn't see it that way.

In New Testament language, the word sufficient means the perfect amount. It was the word used to describe the military solution to an invader who had breached a defensive wall. A massive plug was created that could be inserted in the wall as a perfect fit, so snug and secure that the invader had to start again because there was no way through. That is the grace God gives, the perfect fit for every situation. He gives us exactly what we need, and never stops giving it.

> *His grace is perfect for everything, all the time*

The original Greek word Paul uses for sufficient is also in the perfect tense. It means that His grace is perfect for everything, all the time.

But what form does this grace take? How does it work to build our faith?

For the sake of this session, I will restrict the answers to those things that effect our inner world, mainly because that was the form of grace Paul was receiving in this context. That is not to mean that God doesn't act overtly to heal and alter our worlds visibly, but we will leave that discussion to the next session.

The internal form and function of God's grace is no less impacting than that which can be observed externally. In fact, it could be argued that His work on our unseen worlds is more profound and powerful than any overt miracle.

Interestingly, my observations over many years has been that roughly the same percentage of people actually experience and cooperate with God's inner working in our lives as those who witness regularly His overt and spectacular works.

I tend to put this inner work of the Holy Spirit into two loose categories:

- Spiritual fruit, which we live out predominantly in the realm of the soul (i.e. mind, will, and emotions).

- Spiritual adoption, which is a work done at the level of our spirit or heart.

Spiritual fruit is a form of grace that we relate to quite easily. God works in us so that we might experience His nature in the form of love, joy, peace, patience, and so on – as described in Galatians 5:22. He also gives us tangible strength, encouragement, counsel, and a myriad of other facets of grace that display His enabling power beyond the capacity of our own character.

In Paul's case where God's grace for him was the perfect fit, one can imagine that the grace was particularly in the form of strength, encouragement, peace, and hope. I never cease to be amazed at how much of this type of grace is available, how deep its impact can be, and how far beyond our present experience is the potential resource.

In regards to the grace received at the level of our spirit, so much of it seems to be in the form of relational blessing.

This may seem a strange term, yet if you read some of the prayers and theology of Paul in regard to the work of God's Spirit, so much of it is related to our identity as God's adopted children, and a revelation of His love for us.

Romans 8:15-16 says, "The Spirit you received brought about your adoption to Sonship. And by Him we cry 'Abba, Father.'" The Spirit of God literally and continually testifies to our spirit that we belong to God as His child. When we consciously begin to pray to Him, we are joining a conversation that is already going on at the level of our spirit.

Paul goes on in Ephesians 3:1-19, praying for those who are already doing so well in God that they would have a greater revelation in their spirit of the unfathomable size of the love God has for them. These two forms of grace – adoption and awareness of love – are enough in themselves to alter our lives permanently. Have they been your experience yet?

> *It is this ministry to our inner world that holds the key to experiencing the fullness of God's best for us*

You cannot have the ministry of the Spirit as a part of your experience and not have your faith grow exponentially. It is this ministry to our inner world that holds the key to experiencing the fullness of God's best for us, yet too often it seems to be the aspect of our lives that is embraced last or least.

Somehow we have been led away from the core of God's power and potential in us, leaving only the peripheral busyness of life. Only as we turn to God in faith does the very best of what He has for us begin to transform our lives.

Your Response:

Your daily walk with God is a relationship, not a theory. Spirit and truth are both powerfully developed when we invest in a regular time of reading His word, reflecting on its truth, and talking to Him about its ramifications to our life. This week, before your next small group session, jot down a scripture that you have meditated on in your own devotional times. Then talk through with the group the ways God spoke to you about it and helped you apply it to your life.

[2.4]

Faith to Work

UNTIL THIS POINT, WE have focused on how the rhythm of grace we define as Spirit and Truth grows faith in our inner world. As we keep in step with the Spirit, He empowers the fruit of the Spirit.

Those believers that are more thoughtful and introspective will be drawn to and thrive on this idea of walking with God. They simply love having their inner world full of thoughts and ideas about their Saviour and what He is doing in their life. However, when it comes to intentional evangelism or even working confidently in the gifts of the Spirit, these ones will usually feel a little more awkward.

On the other hand, some people are actually drawn to the idea of overtly witnessing, working in power, and generally being "out there" in their faith expression. They appreciate the deep thinkers, but find it a challenge to relate to them for extended periods.

These two groups are rarely found in the same room. They love the same God but usually aren't drawn to co-exist. That is a shame, because they need each other if either are to come to life fully.

As we have been seeing this week, real fruitfulness comes when we can invest in both walking and working with God. We may always be slightly stronger in one area over the other, yet we need to incorporate both in our lives if our strength is to be maximised.

Our heart of faith is grown when we embrace the rhythm of Spirit and Truth. We can do this in our inner world as well as our outer world, where faith meets life head-on.

This is an issue the 21st-century church needs to embrace more than it ever has. Our society largely doesn't have a worldview that includes the existence of God. In fact, it has gone one step further and feels it has actually out grown the idea of God, and that people who believe in Him are perhaps a little naïve. The evangelism of 40 years ago that was very effective at reviving a latent God-framework in people's minds will not get the same result today.

However, people are still people! In every generation they have a spirit that cries out for eternity and connection with the Creator, even though they have no grid for what that might mean. As God's representatives, we need to seek Him for ways to reach their hearts and break down the belief-blockers to faith.

In our day, that will come about by action more than words. That action can take two forms: that which we do out of faith, and that which we do from faithfulness. Both are valid, both are needed, but neither can be exclusive. All of us are called by God to be involved – whether we are introverted or extroverted, and whether we prefer walking or working with God.

Faithfulness is a natural result of walking with Him. Faithfulness produces a life that demonstrates the fruit of the Spirit. A faithful Christian will engage with the world through intentional and sacrificial love that is given credibility by a life consistent with godly values. Rather than talk, a godly Christian will prefer to listen, since being heard feels so close to being loved that most people can't separate the two.

> **We need to add faith to faithfulness, demonstrating the power of God in people's lives**

A cynical or defensive heart would argue that anyone can give love, not just a Christian. So we need more. We need to add faith to faithfulness, demonstrating the power of God in people's lives. This can seem a little daunting and unnatural to our thinking at first. We know too well that we bring no power personally, yet Jesus expects us to demonstrate the kingdom anyway. Since our mind is often focussed on our lacks, we too easily take our eyes of His abundance. Take heart; even the best of disciples takes a while to get their head straight on this issue.

How do you look at the lunchbox?

The disciples should have known better. They had just seen Jesus feed the five thousand, walk on water, and feed four thousand more. This amazing sequence of events should have been enough to alter anyone's thinking, but it may encourage you to know they still had a way to go.

In Mark Chapter 8:13, we pick up their trail as they get back in their boat just after the most recent feast. There were big things going on. The religious and political world was being shifted all around them, but true to form, their eyes were still fixed on their lunchbox.

Even with all that bread being passed around, they had forgotten to bring enough to last them on their afternoon row across the lake, and this was a big deal. They were male, after all.

As you read this passage, you can almost feel Jesus' temperature rising. What was it going to take for these guys to stop thinking from a place of limitations and lack? They had just seen Him feed four thousand men and their families; what made them think He would let them go hungry now?

He approaches them subtly at first, giving them a chance to self-correct. "Watch out for the leaven of Herod and the Pharisees" (v. 15). These two "leavens" refer to the pervasive effects of humanism and religion. Essentially, Herod and the Pharisees represent an attempt to self-provide and self-justify. Those two mindsets left no room for faith. Jesus was trying to remind the disciples to start their thinking from a place of faith.

But their reaction was hilarious! "Jesus said that because we brought no bread! It's your fault, Peter."

Aware of their discussion, Jesus asked them in Mark 8:17-18, "Why are you (still) talking about having no bread? Do you still not see or understand? Are your hearts hardened? Do you have eyes but fail to see, and ears but fail to hear? And don't you remember?"

He went further. He reminded them of the feeding of five thousand and then the four thousand, asking them how much was left over each time. Then Jesus finished with a question that He may well ask us: "Do you still not understand?"[1]

> *There was no scriptural mandate to multiply food; no written authority to walk on water*

Working in Spirit and Truth

Jesus' miracles were totally outside the grid of existing thought or precedent. There was no scriptural mandate to multiply food; no written authority to walk on water. Jesus routinely broke the mould and thought outside the square

---

[1] Mark 8:21

of conventional thinking. And He was fully expecting the disciples to reason the same way.

He may just as well have said, "Why is your thinking still starting from a focus on what you don't have? After all you have just seen, why can you not reason from the perspective of heaven and unlimited abundance?"

For you and me to begin the journey of working in faith, we need to follow the same well-worn path that the disciples trod. Millions have followed it since then, all equipped with the same determination to get out of their comfort zone. All have also learned in some form or another the power of Spirit and Truth to grow in faith to work with God.

Let's take a few key principles from this passage in Mark 8 and get started! We will start with the Spirit Himself, since He does all the actual work.

The predominant key here is very simple: listen to what God is saying and follow His lead. This was at the core of Jesus' firm word to the disciples. They were focussed on what they lacked, basing reality on that factor. Jesus was trying to have them focus instead on

> *Listen to what God is saying and follow His lead*

the perspective of heaven, where there is no lack. The Spirit of God is seeing things from a place of unlimited potential and creativity. He is not constrained by our traditions or orthodoxy.

The Spirit enables that which He is wanting to do, not what we want Him to do. We are to follow Him and cooperate – blessing what He is blessing. Few things build faith faster than to see the Lord of heaven begin to invade our world to make Himself known.

> **The Spirit enables that which He is wanting to do, not what we want Him to do**

As such, we need to practice listening and following the Spirit's lead and language. He isn't restricted to giving us an "impression" of what He wants us to be working on with Him. He may give visions, dreams, or words of knowledge using the Bible, physical signs, smells, or a plethora of other messages.

It takes some practice, tutoring, and examples to grow in this area. But don't let that stop you! Be prepared to start small, join with some friends, and begin to practice together working with God.

There are many principles here to learn and apply, too much for this session. But the challenge remains to make the firsts steps.

Realigning our Thinking

Just as having the correct idea of truth and reality is crucial to building faith to walk with God, so it is with working. Jesus' rebuke of the disciples in Mark Chapter 8 contains a powerful process for getting our thinking back on track, and away from a focus on what is lacking. He said, "Do you have eyes but fail to see, and ears but fail to hear? And don't you remember?"[2]

Jesus is reminding them that their eyes, ears, and mind need to be aligned with what God is doing if they are to see His great deeds. When working with God, the quickest way to perceive what He is doing is to simply watch. When my team and I minister to people, we try to do so with our eyes open in order to observe what might be happening. It is not always the case, but as we are praying over a person, we will often notice their body responding to the work of the Spirit, either in healing or some other manifestation. We then pray a priestly prayer inviting God to increase His work – to bless that which He is already blessing.

At times, we need to look more broadly to observe God's agenda. This can be done anywhere – on the way to work, at the office, in church, or wherever you encounter people. In those settings, simply become mindful of God and ask if there is anyone He wants you to bless or pray for. When you do this, you will be amazed how often you sense Him highlighting someone, particularly unbelievers!

If you do not see God doing anything, or feel you aren't that perceptive anyway, you can revert to the next phase in Jesus plan: to listen. He said, "Do you have eyes but fail to see ... ears but fail to hear?" If your spiritual eyes are failing,

---

[2] Mark 8:18

start to listen to what He is saying. He can speak to you through His word, words of knowledge, or many other ways. He knows how to get through to you; He has probably been doing so for a long time now. He just wants you to grow in your receptivity.

> *If you can't see and can't hear ... practice remembering*

But what if you feel that you can't see or hear anything from God? Well, that happens to all of us at times. It can dull your faith if you begin to think you are cut off from God. But don't worry, Jesus has a third string to His bow. If you can't see and can't hear ... practice remembering.

Remembrance is a great way to build our faith and focus on the truth that anything is possible in God. Reflect on the times you have seen God work in the past. Remember the amazing things He has done in you and the people you know. Listen to testimony, and grow in your thankfulness for past miracles.

Working in power as a partner with our awesome God is an incredible privilege and a kingdom imperative. We simply cannot leave this central part of our calling to a relatively small number on the radical fringe. By combining Spirit and Truth we can with credibility, sensitivity, and power grow our faith to demonstrate Gods awesome love for the world.

As Paul rightly assumed in First Corinthians 4:20, "The kingdom is not a matter of talk but of power."

Your Response:

There is a key principle to take from this session – our most fruitful work for God comes from us listening and following what He is saying. Our spiritual ears are grown during our time alone with Him. A powerful walk with God produces powerful work with God. What has been one of the most memorable moments when God did something in or through you that only His power could achieve?

[2.5]

Igniting the Engine of Faith

AT SOME POINT, MOST of us experience the feeling of being stuck in life. We feel like our circumstances, history, and options have conspired to lock us in to a reality that we are powerless to change. It might be in regard to your vocation, your church, your relationships (or lack of them), your emotional health, or simply a season of extended trial.

Like an insect caught in a spider's web, the demands of our reality pull us in opposing directions until they effectively cancel each other out and leave us entangled, motionless, and feeling bereft of choice. In those moments, the idea of growing faith, or applying Spirit and Truth seem irrelevant. Even if we wanted to, we don't have the spark we need to get started; our faith tank is empty – too empty to know where to begin.

Jesus defined this state in His parable of the sower. He said there is a type of life that starts in faith, grows somewhat, but then gets entangled by the worries, cares, and riches of this world.[1]

The rhythms of grace such as Spirit and Truth are like a spiritual engine that produce faith. But every engine needs to be started. They need fuel and they need a spark. These sparks come at what might be called "critical moments."

> *Every engine needs to be started. They need fuel and they need a spark.*

In every journey, there are extended times where nothing seems to change too much, but suddenly you hit a fork in the road where a choice needs to be made. That is a critical moment. What you decide there determines how the rest of the journey will look. Will you break through to something new? Or will tomorrow look just like today, only a little more grey?

You may be at such a critical moment right now. Perhaps you have been here before but have not known what to do. Not known there was a choice to make or a moment to seize. Sometimes you can tell it is one of those moments by the questions you ask yourself. Questions like, "Is this what am I prepared to tolerate? What would I give up to change this situation? How long can I do this?"

---

[1] Luke 8:14

The Hunger that Changes Everything

> **Our moments of greatest frustration or anxiety present unique opportunities to reset our path**

These situations come in all shapes and sizes. Our moments of greatest frustration or anxiety present unique opportunities to reset our path – just when most of us would be happy to merely get by!

King David saw many of these opportunities. One in particular serves to illustrate the principle that our points of stress provide catalytic moments to grow faith. A faith that outlives the season that gave birth to it.

First Samuel Chapter 15 tells the tale of when the established king, David, is being threatened by his son, Absalom. The young man had set the people against David through a negative public relations campaign that David had refused to engage in. David was forced to escape the city with a few supporters, back to the hills where he had spent years running from King Saul.

Kings don't flee their powerbase or city without cause. David's life was in mortal danger, and any one of the thousands of negative locals could have ambushed him or reported his whereabouts to his volatile son. David was under deep stress, and fighting off profound disillusionment and despair. His family had turned on him, as had his people and most of the armed forces. As he walked, people pelted the king with rocks and scorn, all because of misrepresentation and slander.

David had no idea how this story would end. The trajectory of events, however, seemed to point towards a tragedy, with David being assassinated at the height of his powers. We see a momentary and honest glimpse into the heart and mind of David written at this very moment. It is Psalm 63. You will probably know some of the phrases.

> You, God, are my God, earnestly I seek you; I thirst for you, my whole being longs for you, in a dry and parched land where there is no water.

> I have seen you in the sanctuary and beheld your power and your glory. Because your love is better than life, my lips will glorify you. I will praise you as long as I live, and in your name I will lift up my hands (Psalm 63:1-4).

There is no asking for a plan of escape here. In fact, no faith for a good outcome appears until the very end of the Psalm. No, David pursues a deeper relationship with his God far more than he seeks rescue or personal vindication.

Look at how this desire is articulated by a man of huge capacity and masculinity – a man among men: "I thirst for you, my whole being longs for you." A man in dire need of faith is instead hungering for God with every cell of his being. Does that sound familiar?

The disciples were told to pray and fast to gain the faith they needed. The Samaritan woman at the well was inducted into the concept of Spirit and Truth. We see David doing reflexively that which incited God to say he was a man after His own heart.

David wasn't told to hunger like this for God; it was written into this worshipping warrior's DNA.

Let me explain. It is hunger to know God that fuels this engine of faith we call Spirit and Truth. You simply cannot omit a personal passion for God's presence from any spiritual equation. You can do all the Christian stuff and yet miss the core completely if you do not stop and develop this side of your life. It is right throughout scripture, but Paul sums it up in First Corinthians 13:2: "If I have the gift of prophecy and can fathom all mysteries and all knowledge, and if I have a faith that can move mountains, but do not have love, I am nothing."

> *It is hunger to know God that fuels this engine of faith we call Spirit and Truth*

Nothing. Zero. Bereft.

That is what we are regardless of all that we do in Jesus' name, unless He is our first love. Stop what you are doing for Him right now if that time should be spent with Him, rather than for Him.

One Small Spark

If hunger is the fuel of faith, then a radically surrendered heart is the spark.

Surrender creates the ultimate critical moment where you and God do business! Hunger will drive us into God's presence, but when we get there, we will be confronted with some polarising truth that demands a response. And that response will inevitably involve surrender.

Surrender takes many forms, but they probably all include the feeling of free-fall.

Take, for example, the moment we give our hearts to Christ in faith. We consciously know we need to give up the rights of our lives, and rely on Him to pay the price we never could for sin. We jump headlong, committed to having Him catch us, and having no Plan B. And He does of course catch us.

But later, when we feel the stress of life and we, like David, simply don't know how it's going to pan out, we are driven to His presence and find ourselves confronted with questions. "Could I cope if my preferred option doesn't materialise? Will I be ok if I am not healed? Can I trust God enough if I lose everything?"

The only viable response is, "I will believe."

Can you say, "I will trust Him no matter what," "He is enough for me without anything else," "His grace is absolutely sufficient"?

Can you trust Him that much?

These are the words of a radically surrendered heart prepared to free-fall with God. And their volume is magnified throughout heaven's corridors and gardens, put on loudspeaker by the angels who have, since creation, been waiting for the answer to the greatest of cosmic questions – is God enough?

Only the radically surrendered heart can scream, "Yes! God alone is enough. I need nothing else!"

> *Only the radically surrendered heart can scream, "Yes! God alone is enough. I need nothing else!"*

It silences Satan's accusations of humanity: "They only worship you because you bless them." It nullifies the cynical commentary of the world that says, "They follow Christ because they need a crutch."

There is no retort to a surrendered heart that has faith in God. It is the ultimate testimony of the reality of God.

Can you imagine for one moment the stress that Abraham felt as he led his long-awaited and only son to the hill, knowing he had to kill Isaac personally? There were no answers available to the inevitable questions. Either God was way beyond the scope of His imagination and logic, or Abraham had imagined the whole thing. Either way, he was committed to find out. As he raised the knife, God stopped him: "It's okay, Abraham! I alone will provide what I ask you to give."[2]

Radical surrender is the ultimate act of faith. And it is something God will call us out on as He determines that we strengthen and grow in our inner world.

> "Without faith it is impossible to please God, because anyone who comes to Him must believe He exists, and that He rewards those who earnestly seek Him" (Hebrews 11:6).

Take Hold of the Baton

Hunger and surrender are emotional and volitional catalysts for faith.

You are a Christian. You carry the spiritual heritage of those who have trodden the path before you and handed you the relay baton. It doesn't belong to the pastor of the megachurch in your city. It doesn't merely belong to the authors of great writings. It belongs to those unrecognised people who hang on to faith, hope, and love ... releasing God's heart day-in-and-day-out to the ordinary people they rub shoulders with on the streets and corridors of life.

---

[2] Genesis 22:12-14

If you don't have faith, you have no life with God. Therefore, build faith. Practice faith. Exhibit faith. We are, after all, people who live by faith from first to last.[3]

Start by searching for and remembering truth – that God is good, His word is true, and He is always sufficient for you. Then embrace His empowering presence – the grace of God applied to your life through His Spirit.

Spirit and Truth. Once that rhythm of grace has begun, it will take you where your mind could never conceive. The world will only be changed for good by a person who is totally committed to God and reliant on Him.

Your Response:

We have seen today that hunger for God and radical surrender combine to kick-start our journey into greater faith. As you contemplate that, is there any other desire that you might be pursuing that stands in opposition to seeking God fully?

Many such personal pursuits are an attempt to find fulfilment outside of our relationship with God. Come before Him now and pray as King David once did: "Search me, God, and know my heart; test me and know my anxious thoughts" (Psalm 139:23). What stands between you and me right now Lord?

---

[3] Romans 1:17

[3.1]

A Hopeful Mind

FEW THINGS IN CREATION are more powerful than a human mind when it is thinking right. Likewise, few things are more destructive than a human mind set on acting out of rage, pain, despair, or brokenness.

In regard to our inner core of faith, hope, and love, we could say that faith finds its home primarily in the human heart, and love demonstrates itself amongst our external world of people ... but hope lives in between those two places. It exists in the realm of our conscious soul. Hope is a way of thinking.

Our mind is the bridge between our seen and unseen worlds, and Christian hope is God's tool for directing how faith and love flow to and from our life. Paul describes it in Colossians 1:5 saying that "faith and love ... spring from the hope stored up for you in heaven." He is saying that because our minds are set on our future state, and on the heavenly realm itself, we can't help but live from a place of godly optimism.

Of the three core elements in our life, hope is understood the least.

THE LANGUAGE OF HEAVEN

Those who live from hope demonstrate more faith and love than those who lack the same optimism. All things being equal, the people who have a high degree of hope see more miracles, more conversions, more peace, and more of everything we might equate to God working within them!

That is because hope is the language of heaven.

> *To believe for the best is quite literally to agree and align with the way God thinks*

To believe for the best is quite literally to agree and align with the way God thinks. This mindset of hope positions us to hear what He is saying and what He is doing. God's logic begins in a place where there is no lack, no anxiety, and no limitations. Literally anything is possible to God. He is never confounded, frustrated, or constrained.

Have you ever found that when you have lost hope about a situation, and you begin to talk to God about how hopeless it is, He doesn't often engage in the conversation? It is not because He agrees with you and is letting you vent – it is because you are using a language He doesn't speak!

Us: "Hey God, can you get me out of this situation? I just can't handle it."

God: Silence

Us: "Lord, it's hopeless. This person will never change. Can you move them on?"

God: No answer.

But if we are brave enough to believe that anything is possible, and that God has a heart to bring life in any situation, the dialogue is starkly different.

Us: "Lord, who in this crowd do you want to bless today?"

God: "Him and her, and them!"

Us: "Father, what is your dream for this workplace and its people?"

God: "Well, now that you have asked ..."

I have never once been in a room of people, and – having asked God who it is He wants to touch – had no answer. Now that makes for a very simple and effective prayer life!

With the two types of dialogue just given, one set has its logic rooted in the Tree of the Knowledge of Good and Evil, the other in the Tree of Life.

The first tree is all about judgement. Judgement defines people and situations based on what is, or what has gone before. It defines the future in terms of the past. It condemns based on performance. For example, if we have experienced repeated disappointment, we become pessimistic because we assume that only disappointment lies ahead. We are projecting the past on to the future, and binding people within that definition.

> **When our logic starts from heaven's perspective, we look for what could be if the limitations were taken away**

The second tree, the Tree of Life, is all about the unlimited potential of eternity. This tree is now rooted in heaven itself, and in Christ we have access to much of what it offers.[1] The New Testament states that we are seated with Christ in the heavenly realms. Our authority and thinking come from heavenly places, and from Christ Himself. When our logic starts from heaven's perspective, we look for what could be if the limitations were taken away. The logic of eternal life doesn't negatively define people or outcomes; it gives hopeful direction. The two are very different.

Definition constrains and measures; it keeps people in a box. Definition says, "You messed up, therefore you are a

---

[1] Revelation 22:2

mess." It says, "You have sinned, therefore you are a sinner." It is judgement of our identity based on our actions.

Direction sets a path to an unlimited future. It says things like, "I see this quality in you. You could become great if you keep growing that!" Direction doesn't confine or limit people, yet it still recognises the reality of what they see in the present.

We get to choose where our logic finds its root – in worldly definition or heavenly direction. Hope looks for the best, believing we have the permission of heaven to pursue that path.

Jesus communicates to us based on what He knows we can be, not on what we have done in the past. He doesn't focus on failure, but on a preferred future. His logic is based on what He can do, not on what we can do without Him.

The Language of Lack

Do you remember our look at the conversation between Jesus and the disciples after the feeding of the five thousand and four thousand? As His disciples focussed on the limited size of their lunchbox (Mark 8:17), Jesus was astounded that the miracles they had just seen had not changed their thinking in any way.

"Why are you talking about having no bread? Do you still not see or understand? Are your hearts hardened?" Using our language, Jesus might say, "Why does your logic still begin with what you don't have, rather than what you know is available?"

His miracles were a sign – a pointer to the ways of God's kingdom. They were also an invitation for His followers to think differently. When God does something amazing, that new standard is to be the low watermark for our faith and reasoning from then on. In other words, the starting place of our faith is the miracles that God has already performed ... and from there the limits are off.

Christian hope gives us theological permission to dream. It isn't merely utopian fantasy or humanistic positive thinking; we are expected to have our reasoning be sourced from a place that has no limits.

> **We are expected to have our reasoning be sourced from a place that has no limits**

Yet where our Father in heaven helps build our dreams, the father of darkness is intent on destroying them. Jesus Himself said in John 10:10, "The thief comes only to steal and kill and destroy; I have come that they may have life, and have it to the full."

If you struggle to hope, and find yourself constantly responding to today's situations from yesterday's hurt, it may be time to recognise how you got to that place. Some people are victims of neglect and abuse in their early years. The victim mindset stays with them, almost as if they are obliged to think that way because it is "who they are." They find it easier to assume they are helpless, or the target of someone else's bad agenda than to plan for success.

Others have been consistently disappointed with life, and remember every dream as being dashed. They develop what looks on the surface to be an admirably stoic resilience when it is merely a sad resolution to endure the pain they know is coming. Many of the descriptors we could use for this type of thinking start with the prefix "dis" – disappointed, disowned, discarded, disconnected, discredited, disinherited, dismayed, disliked, and so on.

To be "dissed" is to have respect taken away. This is part of Satan's plan to steal, kill, and destroy. As children of the King, we are heirs of the family business here on earth. Satan plans to disassemble our rightful inheritance by keeping our rationale blind to our glory and calling in Christ.

> **To be "dissed" is to have respect taken away. This is part of Satan's plan to steal, kill, and destroy.**

Satan does all he can to keep our thinking based in the negativity and failure of our past. When that discouraging mindset is combined with logic based in the Tree of the Knowledge (i.e. judgement) we become boxed and defined by negativity.

By contrast, look at how First Corinthians 3:21-23 expects us to think: "All things are yours, whether it is ... the world or life or death or the present or the future – all are yours, and you are of Christ, and Christ is of God." That is a lot to own! Contemplate for a moment what Paul has said there. Only those in God's own family could possess such things, and that is his point. You are part of God's family – it defines who you are and should control what you think.

> **We don't own the past. What has happened before is wrapped up in God's redemption and purpose**

Yet for everything that is on Paul's list, there is one strategic element missing. We don't own the past. What has happened before is wrapped up in God's redemption and purpose. He alone owns it. You are not allowed to hang on to what you do not own. For those whose names are written in the Book of Life, God chooses to disempower sin and make hopelessness a foreign language. It has no right to determine your thinking.

Seated with Christ

Ephesians 2:6 tells us that "God raised us up with Christ and seated us with him in the heavenly realms in Christ Jesus." You may have wondered what it means to be seated with Christ. It is a statement of legal and spiritual position that means we are identified as redeemed in Christ as well as representatives of Him on earth. Just as an ambassador within an embassy is seen to be in their country of origin even though they are on foreign soil, so are we on earth. An ambassador for the U.S. who is stationed in India is expected to act and think on behalf of his nation of origin.

You are now expected to think like the person Jesus has called you to become. You have no right or obligation to think from the brokenness and limitations of the past. Romans 8:17 says, "We have an obligation, but it is not to the sinful nature." Our obligation, Paul says, is to be empowered by God's Spirit, since we are now His sons and daughters.

> *You have no right or obligation to think from the brokenness and limitations of the past*

As we have previously seen, the Apostle Paul describes two types of Christian – the carnal and the spiritual.[2] The carnal Christian is one who believes in God yet chooses to live as if the Spirit of Christ was not available to empower godly living. Their belief is for redemption but not for revolution of their life. They remain seated in a place of brokenness.

The spiritual Christian is empowered by Christ, able to hear and think from their place next to Him. They see things from heaven's perspective where there is no inevitability of failure or lack. They plan from that place. Though they walk on earth, they are not seated there. They are seated with Christ.

---

[2] 1 Corinthians 3:1-3

Changing chairs is an ongoing journey of critical moments. It is a journey that God is committed to taking us on, and one that is easier if we cooperate. He is our Sanctifier, the One who sets us apart for a holy purpose. It is not just something He does; it is God's very nature to make us holy.

As such, He brings grace to fulfil His purpose. His will is always fulfilled by partnering with His empowering presence. There is a powerful and life-giving rhythm to how He does that. We see it described in one of Jesus' favourite sayings: "The time has come," he said. "The kingdom of God has come near. Repent and believe the good news!" (Mark 1:15).

Repentance and belief. These two elements make up one of the most profound and powerful engines of transformation imaginable. It is our second rhythm of grace, and one that activates a godly hope for the future.

As we begin to unpack the power of this idea over the next few chapters, you will come to realise that in God anything is possible.

Further Reference:

Some of the principles mentioned over the next five chapters are expanded on fully and applied in the Transforming course by the same author, and available at www.kbc.org.au. This eight-week course takes participants on a thorough journey into applying the dynamic of repentance and belief.

Your Response:

You have probably had your fair share of disappointments in life. How greatly has this effected your level of hope in God? Is there any area where you need help to believe that God has a plan for redemption and transformation? How would life look if God actually did intervene in that situation?

[3.2]

An Engine of Change

OUR NATURAL, HUMAN STATE resists change. People don't change unless they have a good reason to do so. Either their present situation is seen to be unacceptable, or the prospects of change so compelling that they will initiate progress towards that place.

Hope is the key to change.

When we see a picture of a preferred future and contrast that with a debilitating present reality, we choose to make a move toward the better future. Don't we?

Not always.

Two things keep people glued to their present:

1. A fear of what they will lose

2. An actual inability to move on

Hope needs to be stronger than both of those things. It needs to include an element of grace. God must give us His empowering presence to do what we can't do on our own. Where we need strength, He must give it; where we need healing, we must embrace it. If we had what it took to overcome the things that hold us captive, we probably would have already overcome them. Clearly, we cannot do it on our own.

You cannot expect a car without gas to get to the pump and fill itself up. It is empty. It needs what it can't give itself.

For many years now, I have seen God bring His grace to revive the stagnant lives of thousands of people, and they are forever different.

However, most people and churches see real transformation so rarely that they no longer expect it, much less plan for it. Instead, they plan for what can be done in their own strength. These people work hard and give sacrificially, labouring for the sake of the gospel, yet few know what it means to have God work through them to produce fruit they could never imagine.

That is not the testimony of the kingdom that Jesus expected. He did not give the Holy Spirit to His early followers – or to us – so that we could go on living as if the price He paid to do that was an end in itself.

We love the cross; it defines all that we stand for. But Jesus is no longer on that cross ... He has moved on! He expects us to embrace the life that the cross made possible. Hebrews 12:2 says that He endured the cross for the joy set before Him, a joy that lives beyond that cross. We are meant to do the same!

God Wants to Break Through

I have seen the ramifications of this played out in a number of churches I have pastored, both large and small. The one good thing that every fellowship has in common is that the people love God and want to see more of His work in their lives and their community.

> *When leaders help their people connect the dots between what is available and what currently is, it is time to hang on!*

This is what God wants too! But when leaders help their people connect the dots between what is available and what currently is, it is time to hang on! Suddenly the church is no longer limited by the capacity of its leaders because the people are being equipped and released by God individually. And He does a much better job of it!

My first experience of this was at a micro level. I had been asked to lead a small group of young adults who loved God but didn't know how to move forward in their faith. We were part of a small-ish but theologically sound fellowship that had no real grid for connecting Spirit and Truth.

As I introduced this group to hopeful and spirit-powered thinking, we began to pray for that reality. Soon, the group began to grow in passion, then in numbers, until about twenty-five people filled our room. We prayed that God would touch each one of us, and the gifts of the Spirit were released wonderfully. Soon, the whole church began to feel the impact of the kingdom. The effect was contagious, and we had to break our group up into five more so the impact would not be constrained. And on it went. Years later, those young people are ministry leaders all over the nation.

When I was recruited to a much larger fellowship, a whole new scale of impact was about to be witnessed. This strong and influential church had for years been rooted in God's Word. Yet they had largely constrained the influence of the Spirit to being a gentle inner work combined with a theoretical concept of the gifts. God didn't want to remove their beautiful reliance on His Word; He simply wanted to add some Spirit to truth!

Many amazing things continue to take place there: hearts are restored to God, missionaries are sent out, gifts of the Spirit are being activated, workplaces are transformed, hearts and bodies are healed, people are saved, ministries are launched – everything a pastor might dream their church would become. And all without anyone working any harder than before.

If any one set of principles could be defined as the difference-maker in that fellowship, it would be the embracing of the symbiotic relationship between repentance and belief.

This may surprise you. After all, most churches teach these ideas. Yet there was something about taking them beyond ideas and into Spirit-empowered reality that broke through.

Making it Work

I mentioned at the start of this session that two things prevent change:

1. A fear of what will be lost

2. An inability to actually move on.

Our greatest breakthroughs take place when people are convinced that these can be solved.

As God began to work powerfully in the lives of a few people who were participating in an experimental discipleship program, the inevitable shackles were raised from those who weren't comfortable with the idea that our church might be turning charismatic. That word was wrongly used to encapsulate a whole range of practices and potential excesses that they thought must surely be in opposition to a strong reliance on God's Word.

Fear and judgement rose to the surface. That combination seldom brings out the best in anyone, so we sought to head-off potential polarising of the church by investing time in transition rather than division. We reassured people that gaining more of one thing did not come at the expense of losing something else. The core of our beliefs would remain intact, but they would gain more impact from God's help.

Some time was spent addressing the false polarity between Spirit and Truth, but much more time was invested in creating safe environments and experiments.

Key influential leaders, staff, and elders began trickling through the program, sometimes very reluctantly. Without fail, they experienced the goodness of God for themselves. We saw the type of spiritual fruit that everybody wants, and that no one could oppose. We stayed correctable and humble in our communication and practice, and this built trust in what God was doing amongst us.

More and more people realised that some changing of their mind was required ... the Bible calls that repentance! That made room in their hearts to believe God could and just might do anything! As we got better at listening to His heart and ideas for His people, He began to do more and more.

> *As we got better at listening to His heart and ideas for His people, He began to do more and more*

If God didn't personally get involved to demonstrate His presence and power, it would have all been a waste of time. If the fellowship wasn't prepared to change their way of thinking, it would have come to nought. Neither repentance nor belief necessarily came first; they both simply started small. Everything in God that stays long starts small.

So Small It Is Personal

What happened at a corporate level in our large church was only as real as it was happening at a personal and granular level as well. Repentance and belief were worked through year after year, in person after person. Not only did we have to explain to them that a preferred future in God is available, but we also had to show the ways in which their current brokenness was unacceptable.

We each become so accustomed to our way of thinking and feeling that even if it is completely dysfunctional, we are drawn to protect it. Home is where you lay your head, and if your mind is in familiar surroundings, it will tend to stay there.

> *Darkness is best cured by light, and Jesus never shows a problem without empowering the solution*

Our curricula dug into the dual ideas of our personal brokenness and the biblical offer of abundant life. This contrast is clear and stark once we see the profound darkness and subtlety that fear, shame, judgment, isolation, and performance have on the human soul. However, darkness is best cured by light, and Jesus never shows a problem without empowering the solution.

We church people are pretty competent at feeling bad about our sin. We say sorry, and promise to quit whatever it is, but in the end we usually go straight back to the old cycle because we don't have what we need to break free.

Symbiosis

Developers of discipleship materials have for decades known of the key phase in our development that transitions us from being carnal to spiritual believers. Essentially, it is a change from trying to live for Jesus, to actually living from Jesus.

James F Engel illustrated this phase with two consecutive steps labelled "Behavioural change" and "Communion with God."[1] The impression from that wording might be that changing behaviour will actually get you closer to God, which isn't quite the case.

What we discovered is that these steps are much more symbiotic than sequential. They work together and rely on each other to find fulfilment. You can't really change behaviour unless you are engaged with God; close proximity with Him will lead you into constant growth and change.

---

[1] Best illustrated in the widely published Engel Scale – James F Engel and Viggo Sorgaard.

What's more, this dynamic is not one that we outgrow. We continue in this rhythm of grace all our lives.

Using the words of Jesus for this rhythm, we essentially Repent and Believe. The behavioural change component is repentance. We identify where we need a correction, submit to God's truth and will on the matter, and determine to change direction in that area.

However, change is impossible on our own. We need grace. And to receive that grace, we need to rely – or lean – on Jesus. In biblical language, to lean on Jesus is to believe or have faith. So we make a godly choice to turn, and engage intimately with God to make that turn ultimately possible. Communion with God and behavioural change are all part of the same process.

As with all the rhythms of grace we can embrace, it is like a spiritual engine that requires fuel and a spark to get it going.

The fuel is always connected to our personal and specific hunger for God Himself. With the dynamic of Repent and Believe, the hunger we require is that of change. We simply must have an actual desire to grow more like Jesus. The absence of that desire will ensure the engine never starts. People who don't want to change will not change.

The spark that sets the rhythm going is humble submission. When we press in to God in the process of becoming like Him, we will be confronted on many issues with the choice to go His way or ours. Obviously, only one response invites God's empowerment, and that is to bow our hearts to Him, saying, "Not my will but yours be done." Personally, I believe a Christian's finest hour is when they are prepared to do and be whatever their Saviour asks of them.

Over the next few sessions, you may well be confronted with such a choice. Will you believe in Him enough to repent?

Your Response:

In the last session you identified an issue in your life that would benefit from God's redemptive power. How much do you really want to address that? If you knew it could change, would you pursue that path? Are you willing to submit again to God's will for your life in that area?

[3.3]

Repenting of Religion

THE WORD RELIGION CONJURES up a world of meaning to most people who hear it. For some it suggests a set of enforced rules, a remote deity, and a certain element of fear. Others are reminded of extremism, war, and an excuse to hate. To others still, the word brings a sense of safety, predictability, and comfort. They appreciate the system of beliefs and actions that give a sense rhythm and eternity to a life that is chaotic and temporal.

Whatever the reaction, the thing to know about religion is that it is a moral and practical framework that, in a Judeo-Christian sense at least, gives some form to the freedom we are designed to enjoy in our relationship with God.

Religion and relationship are, however, two separate things. It is possible to be religious, yet not have a relationship with God – and that is a bad plan. One of the major challenges of having a religious mindset is that the form it presents can actually rob us of the relationship it is supposed to foster.

It may surprise you that Satan does not hate religion; in fact, he has started more than a few. But he does hate people having an intimate relationship with God. He knows that the power, identity, grace, and freedom we seek are all found through personal relationship with God. One of his primary ploys is to replace that relationship and its benefits with pious-looking alternatives that avert our eyes from looking directly at God and veil our hearts from engaging with Him.

> *It may surprise you that Satan does not hate religion; in fact, he has started more than a few*

Good that Robs us of God

Religion can easily play in to the bias we all have for judgement and humanism that come when we live from the Tree of the Knowledge of Good and Evil. It compels us to try to earn favour based on merit and do it in our own strength. In that sense, a religious framework that was meant for good can be the very thing that prevents us from getting to God.

The veil caused by religion was a very real problem in the Apostle Paul's mind. He had been a victim of it himself, and readily saw it in the lives of others. Speaking of those who adhered to the Law as a means of redemption he said the following in Second Corinthians 3:13-17:

> Even to this day when Moses is read, a veil covers their hearts. But whenever anyone turns to the Lord, the veil is taken away. Now the Lord is the Spirit, and where the Spirit of the Lord is, there is freedom.

Paul was offering freedom in the place of form, if it was form that was hindering freedom. Christ's death tore the temple veil that separated God and humanity. But Paul is saying that people can proverbially sew the veil back up again by trying to perform and "play" religion.

What does all this have to do with you? Just this ... you may well have fallen for the worthless trades that Satan offers through an overemphasised religious mindset.

Ask yourself this ... Do you live with a sense of tangible rest, fruit, strength, miraculous power, joy, and encouragement from God personally? If not, there is a good chance that a veil remains between you and God – a veil that you have sewn up.

Don't worry, God still loves you. If you have faith in Him to pay for your sin, you will still get to heaven. But there is a good chance that if you saw the truth of where you fit in the category of carnal verses spiritual, the answer may not be what you expect. Even if you have been serving Him for years.

Let us look again at our anchor verse for this series:

Are you tired? Worn out? Burned out on religion? Come to me. Get away with me and you'll recover your life. I'll show you how to take a real rest. Walk with me and work with me—watch how I do it. Learn the unforced rhythms of grace (Matthew 11:28 – MSG).

Again, notice that this word religion comes up. It is seen here as a load on people's backs that brings fatigue and hopelessness instead of rest and hope.

The Worthless Trades

What exactly does religion offer that robs us of what we need? What is it that we need to repent of? In essence, it is a series of worthless trades that seek to substitute the benefits of an actual relationship with God. All of our needs are intended to be met through engaging intimately with God. Religion can appear to offer valid and more appealing alternatives than this confronting, yet empowering, relationship with our Creator.

> *All of our needs are intended to be met through engaging intimately with God*

Let us look at some of the benefits of relationship with God that can be replaced by worthless trades:

Acceptance

When God created us, we stood before Him naked and unashamed. He looked upon us, eyes wide open, and loved us. Before we had done anything right, God loved. And when we continue to do everything wrong, God still loves us. There is no "because" in why God loves us; it is in His very fabric to do so. When we sinned at the fall, God didn't stop seeing and loving us. He hates sin, but loves the sinner – eyes wide open still. He sees it all and accepts us in Christ.

> *There is no "because" in why God loves us; it is in His very fabric to do so*

Religion would say no to that – it trades acceptance for shame. It says that if and when you fail, you must both hide and make recompense. Religion says that your actions must earn the right to be in God's presence, and that what you do is more important than the state of your heart. A religious spirit will feel guilty, even though it relies on Christ for redemption.

Sonship

The relational context between God and the Christian is that of family. As individuals, we are sons of God (including females). Corporately, we are the Bride of Christ (including males). Gender is irrelevant because these are positional titles that come with privilege and authority.

Religion turns sons to slaves. God is no longer seen as Father, but as a boss who gives orders. Slaves cannot take initiative or exercise choice and wisdom; they wait to be told what to do. Sons are stewards of the family business and go about expanding its influence through faithfulness rather than obligation.

Love

Love goes way beyond conditional acceptance in that love takes the initiative to pursue, embrace, and protect the one who is loved. Love gives and pays a price. Love completes the other person – being strong where they are weak.

Religion exchanges love with hate. Rather than compensate for the failings of others, it sees those failures as an excuse to vilify and separate. Religious thinking forms denominations – pooling together only those who can agree, rather than loving all on the basis of covenant relationship.

Intimacy

There is simply no valid substitute for genuine and interactive communion with God. We are designed with that need woven into us at a cellular level. At the same time, it is the single facet of our walk that is hardest to sustain. Because the urgent needs and activities of our world are visible and loud, we gravitate towards them. The God we cannot see, and who often speaks with an "inside voice," can easily be drowned out.

> **Satan doesn't mind you being busy, even building the kingdom, as long as it disengages you from God Himself**

Satan has a few key ploys here, but his favourite exchange for a Christian's intimacy is activity. He doesn't mind you being busy, even building the kingdom, as long as it disengages you from God Himself. He knows your work will ultimately come to nothing unless you abide fully in Christ. You will inevitably get burned out on religion, and Satan will be there waiting, ready to convince you that the local church is not God's plan for the world.

Eternal Purpose

God made us to enjoy Him and advance His kingdom. Our mandate in Genesis 1:28 was to multiply and bring the earth under the influence of His rule. When we are not doing this God's way, our hearts quickly get restless, looking for meaning in any method that stimulates our desire to make progress.

Satan seeks to divert us from building the kingdom to building our own empire. The switch is often imperceptible, because good people may still be doing good things, but success can draw them away from the purity of their first motives. We can tell when it's about us because we hold our success too tightly, and think that we can do it in our own strength.

Fruit

Every living thing God has made has seeds of multiplication within it. You may have noticed that only man-made fruit has no seeds. The implications of this are very broad, but for this context, the key principle is that fruit comes naturally; it isn't forced. Our "unforced rhythms of grace" all produce their own type of fruit. It comes as an overflow of an abundant inner world that can't help but pour out into every aspect of life. The fruit of the Spirit are like that; they are an outworking of the power of God within.

Satan will replace fruit with religious rules. Religion is focussed on the exterior actions and boundary markers, not the inner heart issues that drive them. It requires us to conform outwardly, even if it fosters inner hypocrisy.

Repenting of Religion

This list is not exhaustive by any means. We have real needs for forgiveness, community, and so on, but I have highlighted a few that directly work to distract us from our primary core – that being faith, hope, and love derived from intimacy with God.

You may have thought that I would list more obvious "sin-like" issues from which to repent. Feel free to do that; you probably know what they are already. My question to you is this – how is all that working out for you? Has your repentance resulted in permanent life-change?

I thought as much.

Our outward and obvious sin is a result of deeper issues such as those mentioned here. Most Christians need to repent of their religion and rely more on (or believe in) their relationship with God.

We are not slaves ... we are sons![1]

This concept alone, when fleshed out and fully embraced, is the single biggest game-changer in spiritual growth. Repentance is, more than anything else, a change in the way we think. When we begin to think as God's children and heirs, we realise that God doesn't want less of us, He actually wants all of us!

When He has that, the limits are off!

Your Response:

Think back again to the area in which you would like to see God bring real change. What thinking needs to change there? What lie about yourself and God might you have bought in to? Most sinful and negative fruit in our life is caused by a corrupt root. What lies at the heart of the problem for you?

---

[1] Galatians 4:6-8

[3.4]

Believing for Today

AS CHRISTIANS, WE SAY sorry to God all the time for the misdeeds we exhibit on a routine basis. It is what we do. Less frequent, though, is a pervasive hope that we won't fail the same way again.

Hope comes from having a preferred future in mind of how life will look for us as we continue in the way of grace. When we don't truly believe real change is possible, we lose that hope. Proverbs 13:12 reminds us, "Hope deferred makes the heart sick, but a longing fulfilled is a tree of life."

Saying sorry is not repentance. Repentance is a change of mind and action; it means to literally switch direction. For repentance to find its fulfilment, our direction needs to be turned toward Jesus.

The best of our own strength and morality is not enough to change our thinking and actions. We need help! The point of New Testament themes such as redemption and Spirit-empowerment are not that God raised the bar on the expectation of your performance. They were to take that burden off your back by having Jesus pay the price once and for all. God has given you His Spirit to increasingly empower you from within to do what was previously unattainable in your own strength.

To fully embrace Jesus' rhythm of Repentance and Belief, we need to understand not only how to do our part of the cycle, but how to let Jesus do His. To do that, we need to practice taking up and handing off the baton of responsibility.

Intersections

At the points where repentance and belief intersect on the cycle, there are critical moments of transition. We normally don't even notice this cycle until there is a sense that something in our life needs to be dealt with. What is occurring at such times is that the Spirit – who has been silently working in you to bring you to life and bring conviction – is now pinpointing a problem.

In Mark 1:15 Jesus said, "The time is now, the kingdom is at hand. Repent and believe." The word "time" in the original text is the Greek word Kairos, meaning "an opportune moment." These moments regularly appear when the Spirit points to an issue needing correction. With that conviction, the power to live God's way is made available to those who seize the moment to repent and rely on God.

The first intersection is the critical "Kairos" moment of conviction. In the cycle, it is the point where the repentance phase begins.

The second critical moment is the handover of responsibility between repentance and belief. By changing our direction and committing to a goal we have no capacity to fulfil, we are exercising faith that God will empower us to do so.

The problem is that those who try to repent without understanding this rhythm of grace commit to doing better in their own strength instead of relying on God. They effectively shortcut the process, bypassing the phase of belief and bisecting the cycle. They go straight back to the start and relive the old pattern they had already been living in.

No wonder our hearts get sick! If we had what it took to change in our own strength, we probably would have by now. What hope is there when we see ourselves repeating that same pattern all our life?

Stepping into Belief

The step from repentance to belief in any area is most powerful when we intend to make the choice just once.

> *It takes a lot more energy to make a decision than it does to manage that decision.*

It takes a lot more energy to make a decision than it does to manage that decision. When we choose to repent of something, we are making the tough call to change direction. That process draws deep from our limited reserves of self-control. Once made, however, we can manage that decision with a lot less effort if the path back to our old behaviour or thinking is no longer open to us.

There is a proverbial bridge between repentance and belief. We need to step over that bridge and then blow it up! We can blow these bridges up by putting in place a mechanism of accountability or practice that makes it difficult to go back. We might, for example, give friends access to our private life, or permission to correct us when we fall back into old behaviours. Ultimately, we need to ensure that reverting to old behaviours would require a price that we don't want to pay.

Now we are ready for a step of faith in Jesus. We are reliant on Him to give us what we can't give ourselves. To do that wisely, it helps to know exactly what the Spirit gives us. Then we aren't having faith in God to do what He never promised to do.

For example, God never said He would take away our lust or greed. We are the stewards of our minds and need to make a choice to not feed those habitual ways of thinking. What He does promise is strength, encouragement, wisdom, healing, and a myriad of other forms of grace that empower us to pursue a higher vision for life. His focus is not on dealing with our old natures; God wants the "old man" within us to stay dead. His intent is on bringing the Spirit-empowered nature to the fore.

The hope that this process develops is at a higher level than merely overcoming sin. God is looking from heaven's perspective and invites you to do the same since you are legally and spiritually seated with Him in heavenly places.[1] Colossians 3:1 says, "Since you have been raised with Christ, set your hearts on things above where Christ is seated at the right hand of God."

This is a much grander vision for life and helps us paint a preferred future for ourselves that brings life and impact wherever we go. Our goal, then, is not to merely avoid the behaviour that brings inner "death by a thousand cuts." It is to come to a full and abundant life.[2]

A Hand at Your Back

It can be a challenge to understand how to live from God's strength instead of your own. He is Spirit, and deals with us primarily at the level of the unseen and intangible. Jesus

---

[1] Ephesians 2:6
[2] Romans 8:13

described it this way: "Whoever believes in me ... rivers of living water will flow from within them."³

That may or may not have been your experience up until now. If not, don't panic. The ability to embrace and walk in the power of God's Spirit can take a little practice! But this is exactly why we need to continually bring our focus back to living in constant union with Christ. After a while it will become normal, not something reserved for mystics.

Indeed, by New Testament definition, to live any other way than being engaged spiritually with God is abnormal. To refute or ignore it is to cut out so much of the New Testament as to make it meaningless.

> *Our role is to determine to walk in His ways; His role is to empower a choice that aligns with His will*

Our role is to determine to walk in His ways; His role is to empower a choice that aligns with His will.

Perhaps I can illustrate the dynamic this way. At the time my wife and I were expecting our first child, we were living next to a beautiful beach. We would walk there often, particularly as the sun set. As she came closer to the big day, she had increasing trouble scaling the sixty or so steps that rose from the sand up to our house.

---

³ John 7:38

She was committed to getting up those stairs, but could not do it on her own. So I would place my hand at her back as she set off, giving her the help she needed to climb. Any more help and she would have fallen over; any less and the climb would have been impossible. The grace she required had to be sufficient – no more, no less.

Does it sound familiar?

God said to the struggling apostle, "My grace is sufficient for you, for my power is made perfect in weakness." Paul responded, "I will boast all the more gladly about my weaknesses, so that Christ's power may rest on me."[4]

We all want Christ's power to rest on us. Often it begins by acknowledging our inability to do what is being asked – by "boasting about weakness." The fact is, everything God calls us to fulfil is impossible in our own strength. "Apart from me you can do nothing," Jesus said.[5]

We sometimes err by thinking, "Well, some of this I can do on my own, and the rest is impossible."

Let me assure you, all of it is impossible!

Jesus told the disciples (and us by the way) to heal the sick, raise the dead, cleanse the leper, and drive out demons.[6]

---

[4] 2 Corinthians 12:9
[5] John 15:5
[6] Matthew 10:8

Now that is definitely impossible. Jesus knew His followers couldn't do that, but He said it anyway.

God also says to be holy as He is holy.[7] That is just as impossible. He doesn't set those things before us to demand an unreachable standard. He does it to invite us to a potential we are unable to imagine. He sets before us a preferred future that requires Him to fulfil it.

His call gives us permission to think and act differently. It is permission to dream, to practice, and to grow.

GRACE FOR EVERYTHING

So what about right now? What about the things you struggle with today – the lust, greed, apathy, grief, trauma, lies, and selfish ambitions? Is there grace we can find for these issues? Of course! God's grace is always the perfect fit.

We start by forming a vision for our life worth aiming for, one where we are not a slave to our old nature. Then, by choosing not to sin and admitting that we have no obligation to it, we create a space in our heart that was previously filled with the insatiable desire for whatever that thing was. The resultant vacuum is filled with God Himself at our invitation. He fills us with His Spirit – the Spirit that, as James says, "envies jealously for us."[8]

---

[7] 1 Peter 1:16; Leviticus 11:44

[8] James 4:5

The Spirit draws our longing towards Him. A heart longing for life has no desire left in it for that which brings death. As we draw near to Him, He draws near to us ... encouraging, strengthening, counselling, purifying, and healing.

Who draws near first? We do; that's the way it works. James 4:8 tells us to draw near to God, and He will draw near to you.

God will not impose Himself upon us. He invites us to love Him in the presence of a choice not to love. That is why there were two trees in the Garden of Eden. God wants fellowship with those who choose to seek Him when there are other options available.

> *He invites us to love Him in the presence of a choice not to love*

He empowers our choice without making that choice for us.

When my wife was looking up at the stairs, it was not the moment for me to lend a hand. I had to wait until she began to step, lest I push her off balance.

We take the first step, knowing that we cannot finish even that without God's hand at our back. That is what it means to believe.

Hope for a better future comes from the amazing rhythm we call Repent and Believe.

Today ... right now, is your "Kairos" time where God invites you into the circle.

It is time to change the way you think and believe in God for more.

Your Response:

2 Peter 1:3 says that God's divine power has given us everything we need for a godly life. What is it then that you need? Is it strength, wisdom, encouragement, or perhaps peace? If you know what you need, and can be sure from scripture that it is God's plan to give it, then you can ask for it with confidence.

[3.5]

Believing for Tomorrow

IN REVELATION 2:17 WE are given a glimpse into the way God determines His plans for us.

Jesus Himself was writing a letter from heaven to the church in Pergamum, a place immersed in satanic ritual and oppression. Right there, in the middle of martyrdom and oppression, God planted a seed that brought a glint back to their eye:

> To the one who is victorious, I will give some of the hidden manna. I will also give that person a white stone with a new name written on it, known only to the one who receives it.

The hidden manna probably refers to experiencing communion with Christ Himself as the bread of life. The white stone was a symbol of legal acquittal, of receiving a "not guilty" verdict. We all get a stone one day, and, interestingly, the stone has a name on it.

Your new name.

A name in biblical culture was connected to identity and character. People were named in such a way as to declare their nature, the circumstances of their birth, or their potential destiny. Old Testament Abram's name meant "exalted father." He was given the name as a baby, yet it was a promise of what was his to become. God renamed him Abraham, meaning "father of nations". Gods idea of his potential far exceeded that of Abrahams' family.

God has a name for you, too. A name which sums up much of what He has built in to you, and who He is calling you to become. That name is already written on your stone in heaven. That is where you are heading, in both location and character. God has already determined who He wants you to become, and His plan is way bigger than yours.

> *Few people spend time considering who it might be that God is calling them to become*

Few people spend time considering who it might be that God is calling them to become. More time is usually spent trying to discover what He plans for us to do.

What we do is a direct result of who we become, thus God's focus is on growing you as a person. He is much more interested in you personally than in anything you might do. And He is obsessively involved in developing you to that end.

We should never mistake God's total love for us as we are as a love that will leave us less than we can be.

Repenting of Equilibrium

The most challenging encounters I have as a pastor are not with cynical unbelievers or those who are going through debilitating hardship. It is dealing with people who refuse to change.

Some people are simply recalcitrant! They are stuck and determined to stay there. And where they are is seldom in a good place.

The reasons behind their immobility may be circumstantial, relational, or even emotional – but whatever the cause, they are suspended in equilibrium.

> ***God does not accept equilibrium as an ultimate state for you***

Equilibrium is a state of zero motion resulting from opposing forces that cancel each other out. Imagine you have a rope tied to each arm and leg, with a horse at the end of each rope pulling away from you. Your first concern at that point is that you not be torn apart. The last thing you want is someone adding more force to one rope just to have you move. In that situation you would do all you can to keep things stable (excuse the pun).

But God does not accept equilibrium as an ultimate state for you. He is determined to call you forward. Either by cutting entanglements or strengthening you, He is intent on getting you moving in some way. And He will do it in a way that results in freedom, not damage.

We see this principle illustrated vividly in God's dealing with His High Priest, Joshua, in Zechariah Chapter 3. Joshua was stuck, as was his fellow leader, Zerubbabel. They were commissioned by God to rebuild the Hebrew temple years after it had been destroyed by invaders and the Jewish people had scattered. It was time to restore worship in Jerusalem.

Due to a combination of difficult circumstances, and a subsequent loss of hope, God's two men had long since given up. For over fifteen years the ruins had lain dormant, mocking the men with its silence. After that length of time they, too, would have become cynical, blaming their failure on others, being ashamed of themselves, and no longer wanting to raise the subject.

But God was not done with Joshua. And He is not done with you.

Look at how He restores hope in a man who is expecting to be judged! God doesn't threaten punishment. He sees Joshua as a stick that is too close to the fire.

> Then he showed me Joshua the high priest standing before the angel of the LORD, and Satan standing at his right side to accuse him. The LORD said to Satan, "The LORD

rebuke you, Satan! The LORD, who has chosen Jerusalem, rebuke you! Is not this man a burning stick snatched from the fire?"

Now Joshua was dressed in filthy clothes as he stood before the angel. The angel said to those who were standing before him, "Take off his filthy clothes." Then he said to Joshua, "See, I have taken away your sin, and I will put fine garments on you" (Zechariah 3:1-4).

It is not God who accuses; it is Satan. And it isn't God that wants us stuck in equilibrium. He continually offers salvation and restoration.

God's intent is that we fulfil our calling, and His Plan A for enacting that process is grace.

> *It is not God who accuses; it is Satan. And it isn't God that wants us stuck in equilibrium*

This theme is right through scripture, consistently reminding us that "God's kindness leads us to repentance."[1] He offers to wash off the mess we ourselves made, and restore the calling He placed on us before that mess ever existed. Then He builds hope ...

---

[1] Romans 2:4

"See, the stone I have set in front of Joshua! There are seven eyes on that one stone, and I will engrave an inscription on it," says the LORD Almighty (Zechariah 3:9).

There is that stone again! A symbol of hope, calling, and God's determination to break our equilibrium.

Buoyed by their renewed call, Joshua and Zerubbabel got back to work, refusing to let their ropes hold them anymore. Eventually, the world will always back down in the face of God and His purpose being fulfilled.

For hope to be restored for our future, we need to repent of the lies we have believed about ourselves and God. We must then find ourselves in Him again through belief.

Connected Calling

> *Hope for our future is not based on shallow optimism*

Hope for our future is not based on shallow optimism. It is based on the reality of our spiritual position as sons who are seated with Christ. But further than that, our hope is found by connecting with the God who makes all things possible.

This is starkly evident in the life of Simon Peter. Throughout Jesus' ministry, Simon had continued to show more zeal than character. He was all over the place! His name meant "reed," something easily bent and blown about by the wind.

One day, right in the midst of his normal string of failures, Jesus publically calls out the gold that He knows is in Simon.

"You are Peter," Jesus said, "and on this rock I will build my church."[2] The name Peter obviously meant "rock." It inferred a stability of character that seemed the opposite of what Simon had demonstrated on a daily basis. Jesus was not defining Simon's destiny in terms of his past failures or present weakness. Jesus defined Simon's future in terms of the potential sown into him at birth. The perspective of heaven always sees more than we could ask or imagine.

Little seems to change immediately in Simon's life. He went on over-promising and under-delivering for a while longer. Still, the call on his life remained based on what God saw as possible. On the night before the crucifixion, Simon declared that even if everyone else fled, he alone would stay with Jesus. Again, his ego was writing cheques that his character couldn't cash-in. By the end of the night, Simon had denied that he even knew Jesus.

Failure.

All the disciples knew it. Simon knew it. Worst of all, it seems, Jesus knew it. Simon had over-reached to the point where he must have wondered if Jesus would accept him back, let alone have him interact with real people ever again.

---

[2] Matthew 16:18

After He rose however, Jesus went straight on the hunt for Simon. Not to punish him, but to restore him.

> **Jesus was treating him according to what he was to become, not what he had demonstrated so far**

One of the first phrases Jesus said at the garden tomb was, "Go tell the disciples, and Peter."[3] Jesus' focus was on the one who was hurting most. And note the name Jesus used – Peter, not Simon. Jesus was treating him according to what he was to become, not what he had demonstrated so far.

Weeks later, the day came to address Peter specifically about his calling. Everyone had been wondering what Jesus would do. As they sat around the breakfast fire, Jesus asked Peter, "Do you love me more than these?"[4]

What could he reply? Peter had originally thought his love for Jesus had no bounds. But now he knew it was weak – well intended but very limited. So he replied, "I love you like a brother."

We often think the point of this story is that Jesus wanted Peter to confess that the love he had was not what he had promised, and that Jesus loved him more. But there is another key theme going on.

---

[3] Mark 16:7
[4] John 21:14-17

Jesus kept re-commissioning Peter by saying, "Feed my lambs." Three times, Peter answered that his love was not what was promised, and three times he was commissioned.

What is the point?

Just this ... our calling is not based on our performance. It is sourced from the relationship we have with God. "Do you love me? Then feed my lambs." This is what Jesus was getting through! He wasn't rebuking Peter; He was giving him the principle that Peter had not yet understood – that our calling is reliant on our relationship with God, not on what we do or don't bring to the table.

Hope for Your Tomorrow

God calls things into being that are not yet visible.[5]

That verse refers to Abraham, who was once called Abram. God changed his name twenty-five years before any evidence of change occurred. He changed his name from one who is head of a household, to one who is a father of nations.

What is God calling you, I wonder?

God is calling out gold in you that you may have no idea exists. This is why Paul says God does more than we can ask or imagine.5 As we repent of the limitations and lies that constrain or define us, we are empowered to believe what

---

[5] Ephesians 3:20

God says about us, even if we struggle to comprehend the implication.

This is hope for tomorrow – and this is your calling.

Your Response:

Have you noticed that God seems intent on developing a specific area in your life? Patience, vision, skills ... love perhaps? He knows where He is taking you and who He has designed for you to become. Look back on your walk with Him so far, what has He been growing in you that you would not have instigated on your own?

[4.1]

Primary Love

WHAT CAUSES A CHURCH that was once flourishing to decay, even to the point where Jesus had to send them a final-notice letter? How could a fellowship started by the Apostle Paul himself – which had seen city-wide impact – atrophy back to near redundancy in just over a generation?

I am talking about the church at Ephesus.

Their simple error is the same one made too easily in our phase of history. They were doing the Christian stuff ... they had been hardworking and faithful, yet they had lost the only thing that mattered.

Love.

Yes, even churches full of godly people can do that. We can fill our diary with good work, but de-emphasise our love for God. Make no mistake however, God does not like it! Doing church without a personal, emotive, worshipful, and prioritised engagement with the Spirit of Christ is a deal-breaker in God's eyes.

Listen to Jesus' words: "I hold this against you. You have forsaken your first love. Consider how far you have fallen! Repent and do the things you did at first. If you do not repent, I will come to you and remove your lampstand from its place."[1]

We need to pause here to consider this point for a moment. It is a sobering warning to a group of people whose whole life was no doubt consumed with their historically significant fellowship. These were Christ-followers, not pagans! Their church had started barely forty years earlier, built the hard way from new converts. They had been lovers of God and His Word; they worked powerfully in the Spirit. Paul wrote them a letter when their faith was booming twelve years into their growth spurt.

What he prayed over them was eternally significant, and it matters to us right now:

> I pray that you, being rooted and established in love, may have power, together with all the Lord's holy people, to grasp how wide and long and high and deep is the love of Christ, and to know this love that surpasses knowledge--that you may be filled to the measure of all the fullness of God.[2]

---

[1] Revelation 2:4-5
[2] Ephesians 3:17-19

The one thing Paul prayed was that they would grasp God's love. He didn't pray that they would know about love, but that they would experience it for themselves. The word Paul uses for "know" is ginosko, a Greek word that goes beyond understanding and into the realm of dynamic experience. It referred to a deep, heartfelt knowledge.

Paul said they needed God's help to grasp this love, but if they could actually get it, it would open the door to all of God's fullness for them. That is a staggering thought. In Paul's eyes, this church already had a lot going for it. But he went for the gold, inviting them to partake in the greatest thing possible, to know God's love.

> ***Paul didn't pray that they would know about love, but that they would experience it for themselves***

Years later Jesus' letter addressed that very issue, pointing out how far they had fallen in this very area. They must have gained so much to have fallen so far.

From Relationship to Religion

What happened in Ephesus is a common dynamic in the Christian world. The founders of any church or denomination usually start out with a genuine, personal encounter with God that deeply impacts their life. At some point they go on to begin a fellowship centred on the shared relationship they have with God.

The next generation is raised up by them to understand and value that same fellowship. They normally adopt the core values and beliefs, yet most have not personally experienced God in the way their parents did. They own the culture that has been passed down, therefore they seek to maintain and even protect that culture with some agreed rules and expectations.

They do what their forefathers did, yet without having experienced God personally or as radically. The third generation normally struggles to find a reason to even follow those rules, and disengages even further.

> *Jesus literally wants to shake down any culture that exists in the place of personal passion for God.*

In His letter, Jesus is addressing this generational issue, telling the people of Ephesus to go back and do what they did at the beginning. And that was to love God radically and personally. Jesus called it their "first" love. It is a word with a double meaning – it meant first in time and first in importance. He wanted their primary love, the very best of their affection.

If you grew up in church or have been a believer for a while, this is an incredibly confronting principle. We normally advocate that our fellowship honours the foundations that made it great and retains that which makes us feel at home. Our style, our activity, and our structure all solidify to embody the personal preferences of the people who are in the room, regardless of the temperature of their love for God.

But Jesus literally wants to shake down any culture that exists in the place of personal passion for God.

Why is Love Primary?

Not only is love for God to be primary in our hearts, but it is also foremost among the three elements of our eternal core. It is what we are to receive, and it is what we are to express to the world:

> And now these three remain: faith, hope and love. But the greatest of these is love (1 Corinthians 13:13).

> Love God, and love your neighbour – all the law hangs on this (Matthew 22:40 – paraphrase mine).

It doesn't get any clearer, does it?

Love is primary because it is centred on relationship, the very thing Jesus died to restore.

Love is primary because – rather than reflecting a moral code – it demonstrates and invites people into the very heart of God Himself. Anything else is just religion.

Love is primary because nothing else transforms a human heart like the sense of belonging, value, and sacrifice that love brings.

> *Nothing else transforms a human heart like the sense of belonging, value, and sacrifice that love brings*

If we stopped all else and did only what positioned us to receive love and give it away – our lives, churches, and communities would be turned upside-down.

So why do we exchange this life-giving connection with Jesus for the endless list of worthless trades the world offers?

Some of it comes down to us buying in to the same satanic lies we see in the Garden of Eden, and also observe during Jesus' forty days of temptation in the wilderness. Satan tries to convince us that we can have the love of the whole world, and it won't impinge on our relationship with God. He whispers that we can have our relationship with God compartmentalised in a box labelled "That's Enough," and still have plenty of our heart left over for the "real" fun of life.

Other more pervasive reasons for leaning away from God are more directly linked with the fall of humanity. Our resultant fear, shame, and performance drivers are rooted in our perceived need to provide for ourselves. We don't trust God enough to give us what we really need.

Our hearts long for security, so we strive to manufacture a life that has wealth and people who will give us what we need. We try to build externally and temporarily that which Jesus offers to meet internally and eternally.

We thrive on significance, but often can't quite grasp the reality of our sonship in Christ, so we trade it for the momentary high we get from recognition or praise. Ultimately, we are trading faith in God's love for fear. We fear sickness, irrelevance, poverty, aloneness, and intimacy – and we will do whatever we can for as long as we live to block out the screams from our heart that demand security.

> **We try to build externally and temporarily that which Jesus offers to meet internally and eternally**

Or perhaps it is something much simpler than all of that for you. Maybe it's just not your style to be too relational with God. You are happy to say quietly that you love Him ... but the way you demonstrate that love is through what you do, not how you relate to Him. Is that you?

Love Received and Given

No human being is your judge. Your connection with God is something you need to work through with Him – personally and honestly.

What I present here is the clear and undeniable message of scripture and of God Himself. He doesn't want what we do if He doesn't have our heart. If what you do is an overflow of an abundant heart, you have accomplished what He is seeking. If what you do is done despite the state of your heart, then you are missing the whole point.

If you need to experience the love of God more fully, but you know your own heart is dry and resisting intimacy with God, then Paul's prayer is still the most powerful remedy. I have seen it change the lives of the most isolated and dusty people.

Pray this daily until you sense God breaking through. Or pray it for those you love who are far from God:

> I pray that out of his glorious riches God would strengthen me with power through his Spirit in my inner being, so that Christ may dwell in my heart through faith.

> And I pray that I, being rooted and established in love, may have power, together with all the Lord's holy people, to grasp how wide and long and high and deep is the love of Christ, and to know this love that surpasses knowledge--that I may be filled to the measure of all the fullness of God (Ephesians 3:16-19).

Only a heart that has received love can give it from pure motives.

When we do receive God's love, it is imperative that we find a way to eventually release it to the world. I say eventually, because love must first do its transformative work in us before we try to give it away. We are not to hand over a package that we have just been handed from God. It doesn't work that way.

First that gift needs to be deposited in us, processed and owned. Then we give away our own heart that has been filled with His love.

Look at what the Apostle John says: "God lives in us and his love is made complete in us."[3] God's love is not complete until it is appropriated within. Then and only then can we give love away. As John goes on to say, "We love because (God) first loved us."[4]

Love that does not give itself away is love that is incomplete.

For the rest of this week, we will see how to grow that love through another unique rhythm of grace. And then we discover God's unchanging plan for where you give it away!

> **Love that does not give itself away is love that is incomplete**

---

[3] 1 John 4:12
[4] 1 John 4:19

Your Response:

What are the things in life that you love the most? List down the top five. But before you, make sure it is the list of "actual" not "aspirational" loves. Aspirational things are those you want to do, or know you should do, without necessarily being what you actually do.

Write the list as if your closest relative or friend, or even God wrote it for you. What would they say are the five things you love most?

[4.2]

Faith and Deeds

When I was a young boy, I remember coming across a wild bunny with its leg trapped in a chicken-wire fence. It had been struggling for some time, and in its sheer panic and wild kicking had actually snapped the bone of its leg. It was in dire need of help, and would die if left alone.

As I approached, it began to kick again, fearing I would bring it further harm. After trying other approaches, I finally had to hold it firmly while I released its leg and bandaged it up. The bunny lived, but it would have certainly died if it had continued to respond from its fear and pain.

Some of us fear the idea of God being too close. Our fallen instinct is to replicate Adam and Eve by hiding from God's presence out of our fear and shame.[1] We are like that injured bunny, running away from the very thing that would save us.

---

[1] Genesis 3:7-8

Fear and shame are powerful drivers; they motivate much of the action and rationale of our lives. For centuries, even Christian religion would use the power of fear and shame to control people's lives and keep order.

> **Instead of control, God's Spirit releases love in our hearts**

But God doesn't control us. He gave us the Spirit of self-control so that we can choose to make godly decisions.[2] Instead of control, God's Spirit releases love in our hearts by the sovereign grace of God. The Spirit of love eradicates those very things that force us to flee.

Romans 5:5 says that we no longer experience shame because the love of God is released in us through the Spirit. First John 4:18 is even more explicit, saying that there is no fear in love because love itself drives that fear away.

Love is the most powerful force in the cosmos. God, who is without limit or fault, is Himself described as love in First John 4:16. If you want to know God, you will be getting to know love. If you are to truly experience God, it will be like swimming in an ocean of acceptance, affirmation, and grace. God does not simply choose to love, He is love.

Shame cannot exist in the presence of acceptance that has no limit. Fear is redundant when the One who is greater than the universe holds us gently in His hand.

---

[2] 2 Timothy 1:7

Overflow

We need to both receive that love, and in due course pass it on to a desperate world. The presence of love is in fact the key indicator of a person that Paul describes as pneumatikos – the Spirit-empowered person.[3]

Despite our fear and shame, there are attitudes we can foster that position us to experience this love. Once that spiritual engine has ignited, God's love is both released in us and ultimately through us to advance the kingdom of God.

In fact, this is God's Plan A for changing the world: love received, and love given away. True love is a sign of Christian maturity. It comes from a sense that all my own needs are so abundantly met in Christ that I have an unlimited resource to give away.

> *This is God's Plan A for changing the world: love received, and love given away*

What drives a person whose every need is met? What do you do when you no longer need to do anything from self-centred motivation?

You go. You walk out the door looking for someone or something that is lacking what you have in abundance. Your personal hunger is no longer a sense of starvation; it is a desire to give away that which is too big to hang on to. That

---

[3] 1 Corinthians 3:1

hunger is the fuel for this spiritual engine. The spark that sets it alight is our willingness to sacrifice.

There comes a defining moment when you are prepared to pay a price for the sake of others. Any price. Love is like that. A parent will not hesitate to run into a burning house to save their children. A desperate lover will pursue their prize at any cost.

A Saviour will allow Himself to be tortured on a cross for the very people who put Him there.

An Engine of Love

The last of our rhythms of grace is the synergistic combination of faith and deeds. These are two elements that cannot reasonably be separated, and they work together to produce a world-transforming love.

The Greek word for faith – *pistis* – suggests that we must lean on what we believe to be true. When I trust in God I am expected to act on that faith, since real faith always has an accompanying deed.

Deeds apart from faith are pointless works. But faith apart from deeds is invalid as well! James 2:17-18 says, "Faith by itself, if it is not accompanied by action, is dead. But someone will say, 'You have faith; I have deeds.' Show me your faith without deeds, and I will show you my faith by my deeds."

Our faith, as we saw in week two of this material, is in God Himself. For those who are empowered by the Spirit, our faith is in the nature of God who is love. We simply know He loves us fully, and that He longs for others to experience that same love.

This belief compels us to look for ways to express that love. However, to ensure those deeds are not merely works done in our own strength, we must perform them with an active dependence on God to provide. Jesus was clear on this, saying, "Without me you can do nothing."[4] Deeds require faith, and faith produces deeds.

One day I was praying for a young woman at one of our spiritual retreats. She hadn't come to seek healing but was enjoying focussed time in God's presence. I was unaware that she had endured six consecutive miscarriages in her attempts to have a child and had for a long time been seeking God for a breakthrough. As I prayed, I was led to break off a spiritual bondage that had come into her family line, and declared permission for her to be healed and conceive a child. Silently, I wondered if that was actually an issue in her life!

It was a statement spoken out in faith, requiring God to do what only He could do. My deed was to speak, and my faith was in Him to do the rest! Indeed, God healed her

---

[4] John 15:5

womb that moment, and she conceived within a couple of weeks. A beautiful baby boy was born in due course, and a little girl soon followed.

Why did God heal that young woman? Because He loved her. My role was simply to be His kingdom priest, stewarding the responsibility of releasing that love.

Deeds of Faith

Faith can be grown. As it grows, our fruit-bearing deeds will naturally expand as well.

> **Faith can be grown. As it grows, our fruit-bearing deeds will naturally expand as well.**

Given that Jesus' rule of engagement stands firm – that all fruit can only come from abiding in Him4 – then the deeds we grow in are those where God's grace is required. Whilst the breadth of possibilities is endless, it is wise to focus our deeds to some degree in accordance with the spiritual gifts God has given us.

Wherever the Spirit of God dwells, anything that God would want to do is inherently possible. However, He gives His people various and specific gifts so that each one can play a part in releasing the love of God. We call them spiritual gifts, but the original Greek word for gifts is charis, which we often translate as grace. They are gifts of grace in that it is God's own empowering presence at work.

The link between our gift-oriented deeds and our level of faith is obvious.

Paul, explaining how to use the gifts, said in Romans 12:6, "We have different gifts, according to the grace given to each of us. If your gift is prophesying, then prophesy in accordance with your faith." To prophecy, or use any of the gifts, we do it in accordance (or in proportion) to our level of faith in God.

This means that if you have the gift of healing but are only beginning to use it, feel free to start small. Pray for your friend's headache, or for back pain. As you see results, your faith increases, inciting you to pray into more significant illness.

It is our responsibility to identify and practice our spiritual gifts. Paul says in Romans 12:6 and First Corinthians 12:7 that each believer has differing gifts. No one has all of them, and no gift is common to all. We are part of a larger body, and if that body is to function properly, it requires every part to do its work.

> *The bigger issue to resolve is this: if the gifts have been given, where are they?*

Logjam

None of this is new. Even though there have been seasons where theological argument and discussion about proper practice has taken place, the gifts are here to stay in this phase of God's story. The bigger issue to resolve is this: if the gifts have been given, where are they?

Do a quick survey of almost any church, asking believers to identify their spiritual gifts and when they last used them, and the silence can be deafening. It is not that the gifts don't exist ... or that people haven't been given them by God's grace. The point is that most people don't know what to do with them.

It is very common to see a spiritual logjam occur in many fellowships. You can observe it along various parts of the discipleship journey. Sometimes people or whole churches get stuck in understanding how to overcome their historical hurts and sin. More common, however, is the logjam caused when disciples are not released into their gifts effectively. Inevitably these local fellowships begin to go stale. They cease to grow because its people are under-challenged and not engaged in ministry.

> *It is very common to see a spiritual logjam occur in many fellowships*

I saw this exemplified and subsequently cured in one of the world's largest churches. While meeting with their inspiring and gifted staff, they explained that at one point their ministries were fully resourced with all the volunteers and staff they needed. As a result of their filled positions, and their lack of need, they ceased challenging people to exercise their gifts in ministry and mission.

Almost immediately, the spiritual health of this church measurably decreased. People became dissatisfied and stalled in their faith. Love was not being released! In their words, they had become guilty of malpractice as a church by not challenging people to reach out in faith.

They soon changed that and focussed again on releasing people in their spiritual gifts. Health and growth returned to the church almost immediately.

Are you stalled or dissatisfied in your spiritual journey? How often are you challenged to rely on God in your deeds of love?

This spiritual engine is available to you. All that is required is your hunger to change the world you live in, and a decision to sacrifice your time, heart, and energy to that end.

> ***They had become guilty of malpractice as a church by not challenging people to reach out in faith***

Your Response:

Do you know where God has gifted you? As part of the Body of Christ your focus on those gifts is vital. Write down your three primary spiritual gifts, or ask a close friend what they believe your gifts may be.

[4.3]

Seasonal Assignments

THERE NEVER SEEMS TO be enough time and energy to take on something new. Life has a way of filling our schedule to the point where we are more often scrambling for a break than looking for added responsibility.

Have you noticed that, no matter what the actual demands are on your life, any vacuum is instantly filled with a barrage of seemingly urgent distractions and options? Our lives can be predominantly busy whilst remaining fruitless.

It is particularly common for younger Christians who get a vision for God's kingdom and who are willing to make huge sacrifices to find themselves in their thirties and forties being energised by a completely different set of values.

What happened?

Well, life happened. Families, mortgages, careers, and dreams of retirement is what happened. In the absence of a grander and more substantive vision, the circumstances of life press in and devour our calendars.

But what happened to the kingdom agenda? Has it proven to be impractical or even naïve? Not at all; the unshakable kingdom of God is always there to be advanced by those forceful enough to take hold of it.[1] Often, however, the next steps for us remain too undefined. We are not sure how to make a difference in our stage of life, or unclear as to which direction has the most potential for us.

Meanwhile, life's more temporal options appear to be quite clearly defined. Our job always has an attractive next step on the ladder; there is a better house within reach for a growing family if we work a little harder; there are holidays we can afford; there are gadgets to consume our interest. The next step is always crystal clear!

Enthusiasm thrives on progress, and modern life will consistently present us with tangible short and long-term measurable gains. And it is amazing how enjoyable and motivating these activities can be. The same thrill we got from seeing a youth group grow can be felt when we get a job promotion. So we might conclude that this is God's best path for us.

> *Enthusiasm thrives on progress*

---

[1] Matthew 11:12

Directing Love

> *The love we have received needs to find practical expression*

In the absence of intentionality, even the most faithful heart can drift. The love we have received needs to find practical expression, and a closer look at scripture reveals four clear settings in which to do that. If approached intentionally, you can have a life of maximum impact wherever you are.

Love the World

In Genesis 1:28, God's standing orders to us were, "Be fruitful and increase in number, fill the earth and subdue it. Rule over the fish of the sea and the birds in the sky over every living creature that moves on the ground." It is part of the blueprint that existed even before the fall of humanity. God had placed humanity in the Garden of Eden, a place that embodied shalom – perfect peace between God, people, and the planet. It was beautiful – perfect in fact – and God walked with them there.

Outside of the garden existed a rugged and uncultivated planet – a blank canvas just waiting for God's people to spread the borders of shalom further afield. We were to love the world by advancing the visible realm of God's kingdom agenda. Our responsibility to govern under the delegated authority of God meant that we were to look after the earth and progress every facet of our society.

This mandate remains. This is our planet to protect, our technology to progress, our art to create, our organisations to build in healthy ways, our society in which to bring peace.

This commandment from God should have an impact on the way you see every environment you engage with, whether it be your vocation, school, or community. Your role there is still to be salt and light. Your presence can advance the causes of God's kingdom, bringing culture and progress in line with the way God would want it. We are to extend the realm of His domain – which is what kingdom means: the king's domain. It is where God's authority is in place.

With that view, how can you take intentional steps in the places where God now has you? Can you make a difference to the relational environment – bringing love where there is discord? Can you bring innovation and godly progress to products and services? Could you minister grace to overloaded mums at the local playgroup? What is your next move forward?

> *Your presence can advance the causes of God's kingdom, bringing culture and progress in line with the way God would want it*

Love God and your Neighbour

When Jesus was asked to identify the most significant of the Old Testament laws, He quoted two:

> "Love the Lord your God with all your heart and with all your soul and with all your mind." This is the first and greatest commandment. And the second is like it: "Love your neighbour as yourself. All the Law and the Prophets hang on these two commandments."[2]

Unlike the call to love the world, these two principles were not stated in Genesis, yet they were implicit in the created order. It was not until after the fall that the things which once were obvious and natural had to be framed as commands.

As we saw in earlier chapters, love for God must be central to absolutely everything we are and do if we are to live fruitfully. But as Jesus makes clear, love for God will always have in its wake a love for other people who are made in His image.

Jesus also pointed out that we are to love others in the same way that we love ourselves. Love received personally is the only love fit to give away. If you cannot embrace God's love and identity in yourself, how can you possibly draw it out in others?

Our neighbours are those we interact with on a daily basis – our community, our family, and our workmates. How can you take an intentional step or have a long-term plan to love them more? How would you show it? How might you help them to embrace it? What do they need that you can give in God's strength?

---

[2] Matthew 22:37-39

Love the Family of Believers

Jesus' life, death, and resurrection was all about redeeming what had been lost from the original created order. He left us with some redemptive commands that ensured the world would continually be reminded of and invited into that story. The first command was this:

> "A new command I give you: Love one another. As I have loved you, so you must love one another."[3]

He was talking to His disciples when He said that – the first body of believers. He went on to say that the love shared among the church would be a light, proving that we are indeed His followers. Intrinsic to the original created order was that people would love each other, but the fall put a halt to that. Now we, as God's chosen people, get to demonstrate a redeemed look at how that love can work.

We are called to love and contribute to the church. We all have a part to play in the proper functioning of the body of believers. If we hold back our gifts, the church pays a heavy price.

> *If we hold back our gifts, the church pays a heavy price.*

As Rick Warren once said, "You can't love the Head without loving His body." Love takes many forms, but none of them are passive. Love always gives.

---

[3] John 13:34

In the church setting, that means you play your part, contributing as God has enabled you with energy and enthusiasm. To love means you actively seek to unify rather than divide. Unity in a church should never be based on agreement, but on bonds of love. Otherwise, at those times when we inevitably do disagree, we take it as permission to divide.

To love in the local church also means you honour the generations that have gone before you, and those who follow after you as well. Love builds up, love cares for, and love embraces those with whom we do not agree.

Love Unreached People

This second redemptive command from Jesus is all about that which Paul described as the ministry of reconciliation.[4] Jesus sent the disciples and us with this command:

> "Go and make disciples of all nations, baptizing them in the name of the Father and of the Son and of the Holy Spirit, and teaching them to obey everything I have commanded you."[5]

Jesus had provided the way for humanity to come back into a relationship with God – the way it was meant to be before we so comprehensively distanced ourselves at the fall.

---

[4] 2 Corinthians 5:18-19
[5] Matthew 28:18-20

Now our job is to give people every opportunity to take up God's offer.

The role goes further than that of evangelising unreached people, however. We are to make disciples – people who become like Jesus. That takes more than a short, mission-oriented trip. It requires relationships and training over extended periods. For many of us in the western context, this mandate also encompasses discipleship work in our own nation.

We are in a society that sees itself as post-Christian in experience, yet it is mostly pre-Christian in understanding. Many believe it is time to move on, to go past the idea of society needing a religious order. In one way they are right; society doesn't need religion. But they are wrong in thinking they do not need a restored relationship with God! Our ministry of reconciliation is needed at home more than it has ever been.

A Green Light for all Seasons

These four specific outlets for God's love are before each of us, yet it would be impossible to make a significant impact in all of them at once.

For every season of life, at least one of these four roads lies before you with an obvious green light from God. At no point does He accept that you cannot change the world for good. If you engage with people anywhere and in any way, you can impact them. If you are confined to a home or prison, you can pray. If you are locked into a rigorous career, you can invest in that environment for good.

When Jesus once walked past a fig tree that bore no fruit, He was so unimpressed that He cursed it.[6] It was clearly not the season to bear fruit and the disciples wondered why Jesus took it so seriously. The point was simple: Jesus reserves the right to expect fruit no matter what the season.

Your current circumstance is – in some way – perfect for bearing fruit for God's work. Like the tree, it is what you are created to do. If you have lost the desire to do that, if the levels of love in your heart are such that you have little to give, admitting that is half the battle. Be honest before God and ask Him to fill you. But whatever you do, do not accept the lie that your life has no calling and purpose in God right now.

The lights are green! Go. Get started. Pass on the love that Jesus gave you access to at the cross.

Your Response:

Of the four mandates just mentioned, which might be the area of focus that God has positioned you for the currently? Enthusiasm thrives on intentionality ... what could be your next step in the direction you see?

---

[6] Mark 11:13-14

[4.4]

Rest for the Weary

ONE NEED ONLY GLANCE at the ramifications and possibilities of the four outlets for God's love that He has placed before us to experience a degree of trepidation.

Knowledge comes with responsibility, and once we understand that our purpose for living is to love Him and extend that love outwards, we have some choices to make. The choices invariably come with questions: What price should be paid? Which way do I go? How much more can I realistically do?

This is exactly why we need to consider both walking and working when reconfiguring our life in response to God's Word. Those committed to going and doing are often the first to lose the joy of God in their life. This is often because they overreach their inner capacity to give and receive love.

Receiving the love we need is best done sustainably in a posture of inner rest. When our heart is in turmoil or rush, it simply can't pause to embrace and enjoy God's grace. God won't impose on us. He will not invade your day, demanding that you stop and receive. He engages with those who genuinely long to engage with Him.

For those who actually do stop long enough, there is a deep well of insight, healing, inspiration, and grace. There are ideas and initiatives that are gained only by those whose pace is slow, and whose eyes can first look up, then look in, then look out.

An Example from the Wilderness

There had come a day when it all seemed too much for Moses.

Even though God had prepared him for eighty (yes, eighty!) years. Even though he had been undeniably called at the burning bush. Even though he had seen God do mind-numbing miracles and extracted millions of people through the dry Red Sea floor – despite all that, the thought of leading these people was too much to bear.

He needed God's reassurance of support. Again.

He had seen God's works, just as the rest of the nation had. But the leader in Moses needed to see more. He wanted to look behind the curtain and see how God pulled the strings. So Moses asked God to show him His ways.

It was an interesting request, one we might perceive as presumptuous or arrogant. But God didn't see it that way, and indulged Moses just a little. Psalm 103 says that Israel saw God's works, but Moses saw His ways. Moses was going to be let in on some of the "how and why" of God's plan.

"My Presence will go with you," God said, "and I will give you rest."[1] That little couplet was God's plan. It was another of those rhythms of grace – presence and rest.

The presence element was pretty straightforward. That was what took place when Moses' staff came out ... big things happened. Seas parted; rivers turned to blood; frogs invaded cities and so on. God's proximity and power would do all the heavy lifting for Moses. He just needed to obey and get out of the way.

God's promise of His imminent presence with us has been re-confirmed over and again in scripture. He really does want us to be aware that He is by our side for the long haul. That gives us is permission to hope, and incentive to plan. We can invest in growing and cultivating the seeds of potential that lie within. We can dare to dream, knowing that God's unlimited support is for us.

> **We can dare to dream, knowing that God's unlimited support is for us**

---

[1] Exodus 33:14

Sabbath

Even though God did the real work, Moses and the people would still get tired. Just walking in the desert year after year was enough to weary their body and soul. So God also promised and provided rest.

If we are overworked and overstressed to the point where we or our family are under excessive strain, something is out of order. God didn't design that scenario; He has made room for us to rest. And rest we should take!

Hebrews 4:9-10 says, "There remains a Sabbath-rest for the people of God; for anyone who enters God's rest also rests from their works, just as God did from his."

> *Rest gives us a moment to draw a proverbial line under our day, and declare by faith that it is good*

Yes, even God rested. Was He tired? No, His power has no limit. Yet this verse, which refers to God's rest in Genesis 2:2, highlights that God paused after His work that was in every way "very good."[2]

Rest gives us a moment to draw a proverbial line under our day, and declare by faith that it is good. Unlike God, our efforts are never perfect, but we can have faith that God makes up for what is lacking in our life and effort.

---

[2] Genesis 1:31

Indeed, it is our efforts that we need to rest from the most. Efforts to be good enough; efforts to meet others' expectations; efforts to find meaning and peace; efforts to achieve something of significance; efforts to please God.

These efforts are sometimes driven by a sense of inner pressure, a subtle obligation to do and be what is expected or admired. Our innate bias to self-judge continually reminds us that we fall short. Even if we cease activity altogether, we are still unable to rest because our inner critique continues to haunt us.

Sabbath rest is not primarily aimed at doing nothing; it is a pause that lets us engage anew with God and agree with Him when He says, "It is good." We are permitted to stop, to fail even, since it is inevitable that we will. Sabbath allows us to breathe when the waves of self-accusation come, because we have faith that God's grace silences every accuser.

This is why Jesus went to war with the Pharisees over the issue of Sabbath. They accused Him of working on what was a sacred day.[3] They actually seemed to have Him there... Jesus was at fault according what Moses had commanded. But Jesus argued from a higher place, drawing from the principle that had birthed that Law.

> "The Sabbath was made for man, not man for the Sabbath."[4]

---

[3] Mark 2:23-28
[4] Mark 2:27

His point was that God ordained rest because He knew our souls could never self-initiate it. The Pharisees had converted something made to bring life into a law that brought death.

A Cure for Restlessness

Rest is the antidote to two conditions. The first is that of being weary. The second condition is different entirely; rest is the antidote to being restless.

Restlessness forms its own kind of weariness, but it is the weariness born of battling constraint. Restlessness needs things to change externally before it can find peace. As such, it only finds a false peace because it is circumstantial.

God's rest comes from an internal peace that is substantial. It is a foundation that lies beneath all circumstance, giving stability to our soul. Any wind may blow, any wave might break over us, but God's peace means we remain immovable.

Jesus once coached the disciples when their hearts were becoming increasingly agitated at His leaving. "A time ... has come when you will be scattered, each to your own home. ... I have told you these things, so that in me you may have peace. In this world you will have trouble. But take heart! I have overcome the world."[5]

I have witnessed this sort of peace that Jesus offered. Perhaps you have, too.

---

[5] John 16:32-33

I have seen it in the eyes of a young wife who tragically lost her husband, the father of their young children.

I have heard it in the voice of a dear friend who had, just minutes before, been abducted and raped. She almost sang, "They can abuse my body but they cannot harm my soul."

I have felt it in the hand of a dying man as he knew he would be meeting Jesus that day.

We have permission to find rest from the need for life to get better.

Yet there is another form of restlessness that is steadily increasing in our culture. That is the restlessness of ambition. This inner turmoil springs from a sense of entitlement, a claim on our perceived right for more. Entitlement says, "I know something more is out there for me. I deserve it, and I can't be happy until I get it." Happiness continues to escape them because entitlement is never satisfied.

> *We have permission to find rest from the need for life to get better*

This type of restlessness bars shut the door to one of the most profound aspects of living in God's calling – that of metron.

Go Deep and Wide

Metron is the Greek word used by Paul in describing the scope of his ministry. It means a boundary or sphere of influence and authority. Paul never sought to increase his influence by scaling higher; he chose to dig deeper and spread wider.

Listen to what he says to the Corinthian church about this: "(We) confine our boasting to the sphere of service God himself has assigned to us, a sphere that also includes you. ... Our hope is that, as your faith continues to grow, our sphere of activity among you will greatly expand."[6]

> *The sort of increase that God wants to grant can only be stewarded by those who no longer need it*

That word translated as sphere is metron – a boundary of authority given by God. Paul hoped for a broader metron, but that was not his focus. His only goal was to bury himself deeper into Christ. He later said of his time in Corinth, "I resolved to know nothing while I was with you except Jesus Christ and him crucified."[7]

There is a kingdom principle at play here that delivers what a restless heart would want. But it only becomes available when the restlessness is gone!

---

[6] 2 Corinthians 10:13-15 (abbreviation mine)
[7] 1 Corinthians 2:2

Restlessness is looking for increase and change. But the sort of increase that God wants to grant can only be stewarded by those who no longer need it. He wants us to have our needs met fully in Him alone, as Paul did. The humility that keeps us focussed on Christ is the same humility that qualifies us to handle more responsibility in God.

Personal ambition and entitlement can see from only one perspective. It looks from its present position with its eyes pointing to a loftier prize. It sees progress as a ladder with one further step ever before it. Humility looks at Christ alone, and the humble want only to be found in Christ. The impact of such a perspective is real, growing, and eternal. It brings a life of true fruitfulness born of rest.

By digging deeper into Christ, we dig further into the purpose and place He has us in. We get more proficient in what we do there, and our influence begins to grow through credibility and longevity. Our going deep results in us going wide.

> **By digging deeper into Christ, we dig further into the purpose and place He has us in**

True rest and purpose are only found when we are found fully in Christ. He is our rest.

The preparation for working is the practice of walking. As we learn to enjoy God above all things, most of the questions we ask from a place of weariness and restlessness cease to matter.

Your Response:

Are you weary or restless? Both are conditions that atrophy our soul. What is it that has drained you?

For every drain, there simply must be a complimentary replenishment, otherwise some form of death is imminent. What do you need that will fill your soul again?

[4.5]

Crossing Jordan

JOSHUA WAS A DIFFERENT breed than most. He had been with Moses since the beginning, but now his leader was gone. Things would never be the same again. Only Joshua and his old friend, Caleb, had made it through forty years of lessons while dreaming of the Promised Land God had called them to.

Many others had been called. Millions, in fact. But from that original population, only these two crossed the river and made it to their chosen destiny. The faith that qualified them to walk into the Promised Land was the same faith that made them stick out painfully forty years earlier. No one else had been prepared to trust God for what He had promised.

God has a calling on your life too. But a calling comes with no guarantee of being chosen.[1] The calling is an offer, not

---

[1] Matthew 22:14

an order. It is a direction you have been designed for, and one that will bring great blessing to you and the world. But calling requires your cooperation before it can be fulfilled. God is with you every step, helping you progress. But if you choose to stop, He won't force you onward.

The whole nation of Israel had been called. Only two walked in to the Promised Land. Centuries later, Paul wrote that what happened in the forty years between the call and the fulfilled destiny serves as an example to you and me, so that we could learn from their mistakes.[2]

LESSONS FROM THE WILDERNESS

> *You have met Him now, and you are ruined for the world*

When the Hebrews left their slavery in Egypt, there was no going back. They were baptised into Moses through the Red Sea.[3] You, too, have crossed over. There is no returning to a life without Christ. You have met Him now, and you are ruined for the world.

The Israelites were no longer slaves, but they still reasoned as if they were. They needed to be told what to do, and given a standard to reach. That's why they were given the Law, lest in their new freedom they would go wild.

---

[2] 1 Corinthians 10:11
[3] 1 Corinthians 10:2

That mindset, however, was never going to cut it in the Promised Land, as was seen only weeks after they escaped Egypt. They were on the doorstep of the land that had been so long promised, yet they refused to go in. They were stalled.[4]

To enter the land was impossible in human terms. There were giants and hardships to contend with. But that was the whole point. God calls us to a life that is impossible without Him, hence the need for faith.

Between the calling and our Promised Land, there needs to be a wilderness season. Jesus had one – forty days. The Hebrews had one – forty years. The lessons are generally the same, but the length of the wilderness depends entirely on our ability to grow and obey. We simply cannot enter our Promised Land until we are ready.

> **The length of the wilderness depends entirely on our ability to grow and obey**

For us, the Promised Land is not a physical place we move to. Nor is it a ministry or job description. It is a state of being; it is your character. Ultimately, it is the fulfilment of the name God has for you. Your calling is to become all that the name really means. Along the way, there are assignments and seasons that both grow you and impact others.

There are a number of significant points of grace along the journey that are like crossing a new point of no return.

---

[4] Numbers 13-14

They are moments when you know something has taken place in you that is transformational. Your conversion is like that. You have crossed over from death to life, and there is no going back.

> *Like the Hebrews, you have inevitably brought your baggage with you*

Like the Hebrews, however, you have inevitably brought your baggage with you. The old mindsets and habits do not disappear automatically. God needs to replace them with a new core – faith, hope, and love. So the wilderness becomes our teacher, and our role is to become students.

The wilderness is nothing like our Promised Land, yet it doesn't need to be a literal desert experience as it was for the Hebrews. It is meant to be a place of blessing and growth.

Personally, I love the wilderness! The real one, that is, where you can immerse yourself in nature. It is where you can commune with God silently or even noisily in worship and prayer.

God says of the season in which He drew Israel into that place: "Therefore I am now going to allure her; I will lead her into the wilderness and speak tenderly to her. There I will give her back her vineyards, and will make the Valley of Achor a door of hope. There she will respond as in the days of her youth, as in the day she came up out of Egypt."[5]

---
[5] Hosea 2:14-15

In the wilderness, we commune with God in a way that transforms us. Note the phrase where God converts Achor, meaning trouble, into a door of hope. That is one of the transformational moments you will recognise on the journey, along with faith and love. Let's lay this out again so it remains clear.

Faith

The moment you place your faith in Christ, it is like crossing the Red Sea. The Spirit prepared your heart and revealed Christ to you. You recognise the truth of who Jesus is and what He has done, and the fruit of that rhythm of grace is faith. The engine of Spirit and Truth never ceases, of course. You need to grow that faith for the rest of your life as each new assignment and season is embraced.

We begin with a faith that God will work for us. His plan, though, is to work with us. Faith needs to morph from a slave-oriented and helpless place into one where we, as God's chosen children, walk and work with Him as friends and partners.

When we begin our journey of consciously walking with God, we are still largely driven by the remnants of our old nature. Paul referred to this stage as being infants in Christ. He also used the word carnal, which essentially means to be worldly or driven by the flesh.

Hope

The next phase of growth is needed to get us past the point of being stalled. As long as we hang on to our old ways, we can't embrace the perspective of heaven and adopt hope for a preferred future.

We need to begin the transition from being carnal to spiritual. This requires the joining of two dynamics – communion with God and behavioural growth.

We are to go from a place of knowing about God, to one of experiencing Him more deeply and intimately. To be frank, some Christians never make it to this point. Because of their brokenness, they are not prepared to leave behind their hurts and pain. As such, they are out of step with the Spirit of hope.

Repentance and Belief is the rhythm of grace needed here. We turn from old ways of thinking and lean on God to empower better choices. Our progress results in a wonderful hope for what will be in Christ as we grow past the mindset of a spiritual slave.

> *A son reasons from a place of family abundance and blessing*

It is in this phase that we embrace the mind of a son. That is a positional term, by the way, not one of gender. A son reasons from a place of family abundance and blessing. A slave reasons from a position of lack and punishment.

Galatians 4:6-7 says, "Because you are his sons, God sent the Spirit of his Son into our hearts, the Spirit who calls out, 'Abba, Father.'" You are no longer a slave, but God's child; since you are His child, God has made you an heir.

It is in this phase that we become much more tangibly empowered by the Spirit. We cease to focus inward and – aware of the abundance within – we turn our eyes to grander themes.

Love

There are a number of ways that experts in spiritual development have defined this next phase of character.

Essentially it is one where pilgrims grapple with the concepts of stewardship and spiritual reproduction.[6] They consider the wealth of blessing they hold within and look for healthy ways to release it. Spiritual gifts are recognised and developed, a revelation of love is embraced, and a demonstration of love is exhibited.

> *This is what King David called a spacious place, one without limits or the need for overregulation*

Faith and Deeds becomes the new rhythm of grace here. We partner with Christ by relying on

---

[6] Best illustrated in the widely published Engel Scale – James F Engel and Viggo Sorgaard.

His strength to work through us in miraculous ways that bear great fruit.

For me, this is what the Promised Land is all about. It is what King David called a spacious place, one without limits or the need for overregulation.[7] That which was once a command becomes a natural fruit. Law has been replaced by Spirit.

Before you know it, the wilderness season has become a memory. Even though you might have experienced some pain and change, there is no regret.

The Promised Land for you is the place where you are living in your calling. It is not that you have arrived at any particular point, or that new assignments and growth aren't still on the way, but you are walking and working with God as you journey on.

> *Calling isn't a place or position; it is a condition of the heart*

Calling isn't a place or position; it is a condition of the heart. It is a state of peace beyond understanding,[8] of love received and given,[9] and of fruitfulness that comes from abiding in Christ.[10]

---

[7] Psalm 31:8
[8] Philippians 4:7
[9] Ephesians 3:16-19
[10] John 15:5

The One Thing that Matters

Few people achieved more for God than Joshua in the Old Testament. He crossed over to the Promised Land, worked hard with God, and took hold of that which was promised.

Moses had been an awesome leader, but in the end he, too, had failed.[11] Joshua did not. Moses' mistake was failing to heed God's guidance and trust Him. Joshua listened and obeyed with boldness.

Where did Joshua get such character? We can see from a single verse – Exodus 33:11: "The Lord would speak to Moses face to face, as one speaks to a friend. Then Moses would return to camp, but his young aide Joshua son of Nun did not leave the tent." Where Moses would leave God's presence, Joshua lingered privately. I wonder how many years he spent doing this.

Every principle outlined in this material has returned to this one idea: genuine seeking and reliance on God's presence is the single biggest key to a fruitful life.

He will teach you what you need to know, guide you in where to go, and provide for you what you need to overcome. If you follow His voice, one day you will also stand on the bank of the Jordan, ready to cross over. So much will make sense from that standpoint. The lessons, the testing, the growing ... the need for faith.

---

[11] Numbers 20:11-12

Perhaps you have already crossed over. If you have, welcome home! Your task now is to bear great fruit by helping as many people as you can take their own journey. There is no greater joy.

This brief writing simply skims the surface of the deep and profound mystery that is your developing life with Christ. It points to principles you will need to investigate and apply further.

My prayer is that – no matter where you are on that journey – you turn to Christ in deep faith. No matter what lies ahead, He is always with you. When you can do that, you are living in His perfect will for you right now.

Go now ... walk with Him and work with Him. Watch how Jesus does it – learn the unforced rhythms of grace.

Your Response:

Where do you believe you are at on your spiritual journey in regard to faith, hope and love? Are you at the beginning; in a worshipful wilderness; or in your Promised Land? Faith, hope and love belong in all of those places of course, it is just a matter of which one rises to the surface at different times. Describe the season that God has you in right now, and what He is growing in you.

Unlocking the Rhythms of Grace

Patrick A. Hegarty

More like this at:
hegarty.com.au

www.ingramcontent.com/pod-product-compliance
Lightning Source LLC
Chambersburg PA
CBHW071237080526
44587CB00013BA/1649